20 WAYS TO DRAW A BIKE

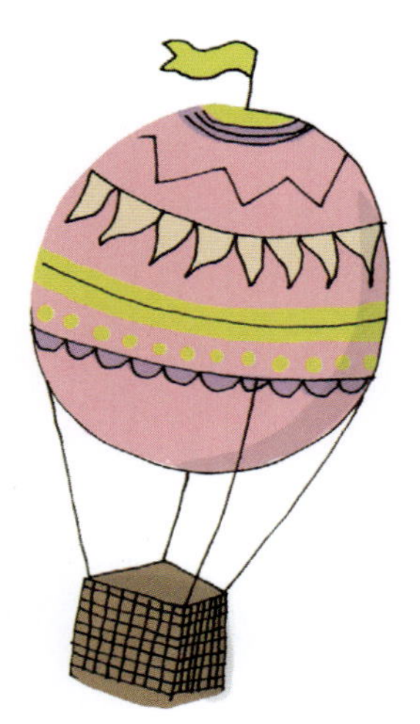

AND 44 OTHER INCREDIBLE WAYS TO GET AROUND

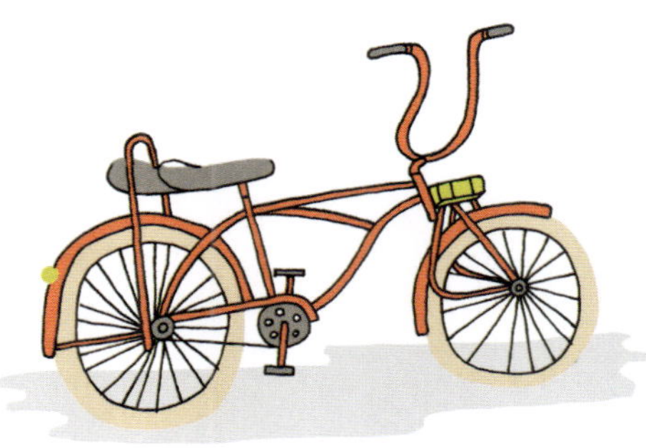

JAMES GULLIVER HANCOCK

A Sketchbook for Artists, Designers, and Doodlers

Quarry Books
100 Cummings Center, Suite 406L
Beverly, MA 01915

quarrybooks.com • www.craftside.net

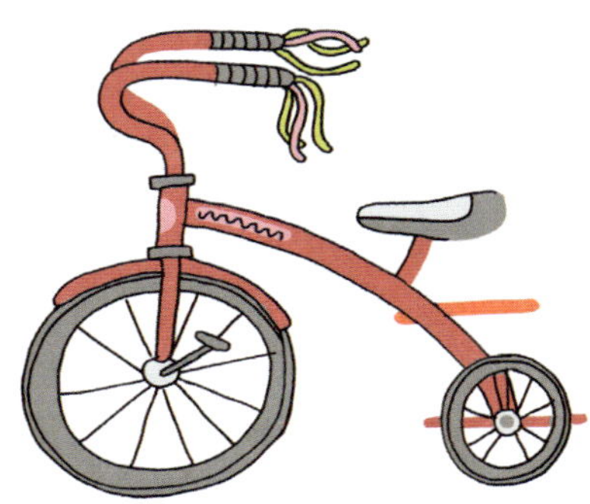

© 2015 by Quarry Books
Illustrations © 2015 James Gulliver Hancock

First published in the United States of America in 2015 by
Quarry Books, a member of
Quarto Publishing Group USA Inc.
100 Cummings Center
Suite 406-L
Beverly, Massachusetts 01915-6101
Telephone: (978) 282-9590
Fax: (978) 283-2742
www.quarrybooks.com
Visit www.Craftside.Typepad.com for a behind-the-scenes peek
at our crafty world!

10 9 8 7 6 5 4 3 2 1

ISBN: 978-1-63159-044-3

Design: Debbie Berne

Printed in China

CONTENTS

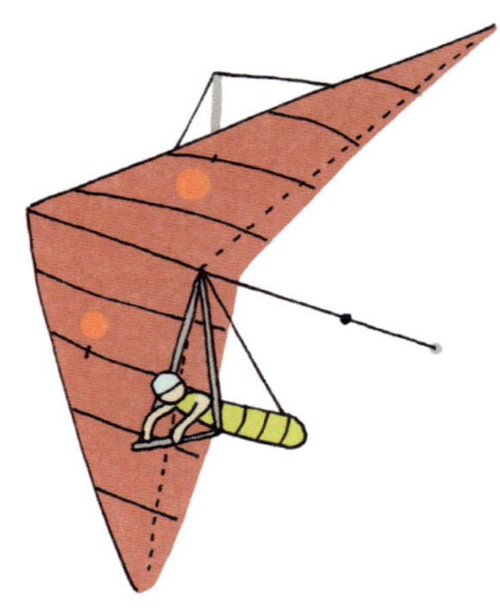

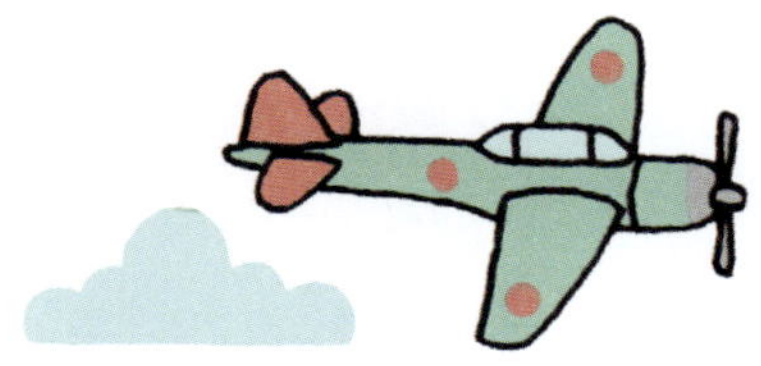

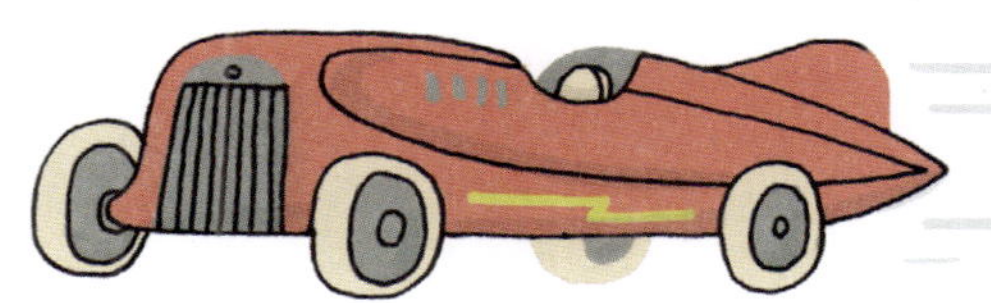

INTRODUCTION

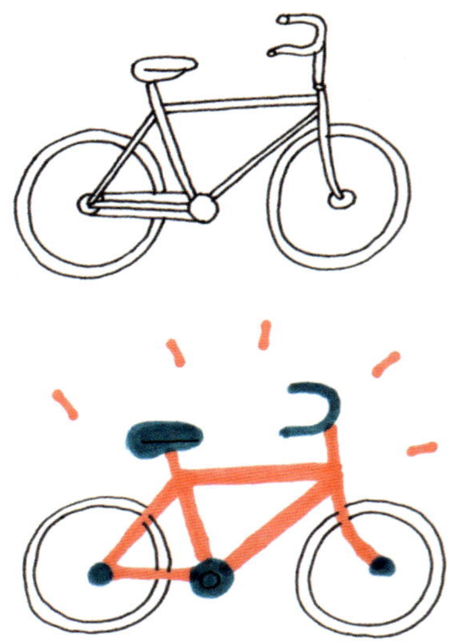

bikes: pen and marker

20 Ways to Draw a Bike and 44 Other Incredible Ways to Get Around is a celebration of transportation and is designed to help you observe, see, and draw in a fun and interactive way. There are forty-five different themes throughout the book, each one exploring a different way to travel, from bikes and boats to scooters and surfboards. This book will challenge you to look at the varied lines, marks, and shapes that bring these items to life and will give you ideas on how to approach your own drawings.

While I was drawing these pages, I imagined all the fabulous adventures I could have while strolling, flying, or skating around. I have always been fascinated by inventions, mechanics, and movement and many of these ideas may come into play as you begin to make drawings in this book. Choose different and fun materials with which to draw. Try fine-line markers, colored pencils, or anything that feels good in your hand and on the page.

It may seem a little challenging to find twenty different ways to draw a bike, but when you break it down to the different parts and shapes and examine all the aspects of this simple engineering wonder, it all becomes fun and interesting. Before you know it, you will have drawn twenty examples. If you approach drawing in this analytical way it will become second nature. Don't feel you have to stop at twenty either. Carry on for as long as you like!

In addition to line, texture, and shape, be sure to think about scale, while you draw. This can produce some stunning results. For example, seeing a submarine from the side next to a view from the front creates a beautiful relationship on the page. Don't miss the subtle details, the not-so-obvious views, and the simple shapes. All of these observations will help you to create fascinating drawings.

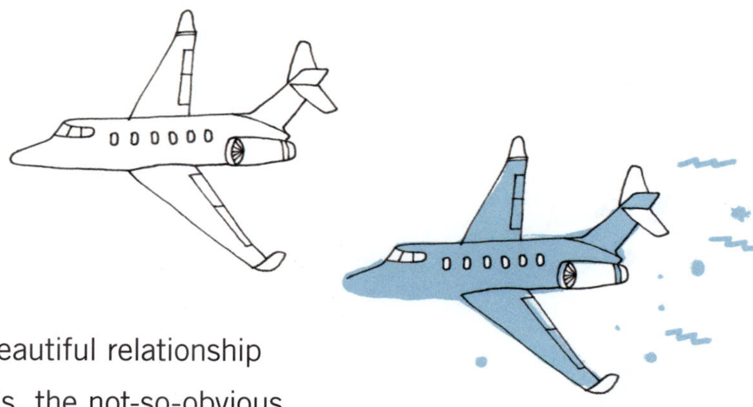

airplanes: brush, ink, and pen

HOW TO USE THIS BOOK

There are forty-five modes of transportation in this book and each one contains twenty examples, all drawn in a different way. Some spreads may have all of the drawings on one page leaving the other page free for you to fill with your own drawings. Some pages have spaces in between to add your own drawings.

Start with your own bike or scooter or car—or draw your friend's. Look at these drawings for ideas, or draw the vehicles you imagine in your head. Visit a train yard or a bus stop and bring your sketchpad along. Remember that there is no right or wrong way to work in this book. Just do it. Don't worry about mistakes! The most important thing is to have fun!

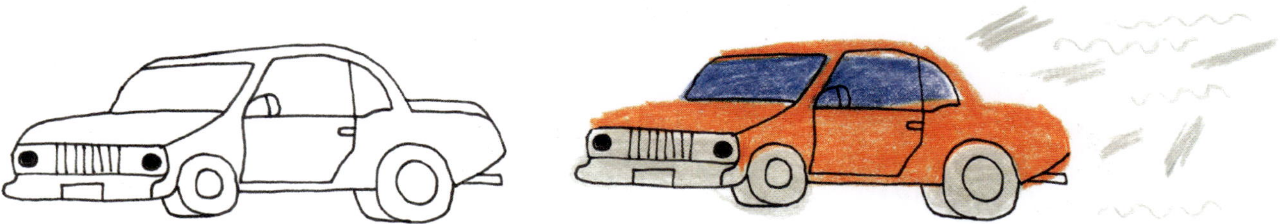

cars: pen and colored pencil

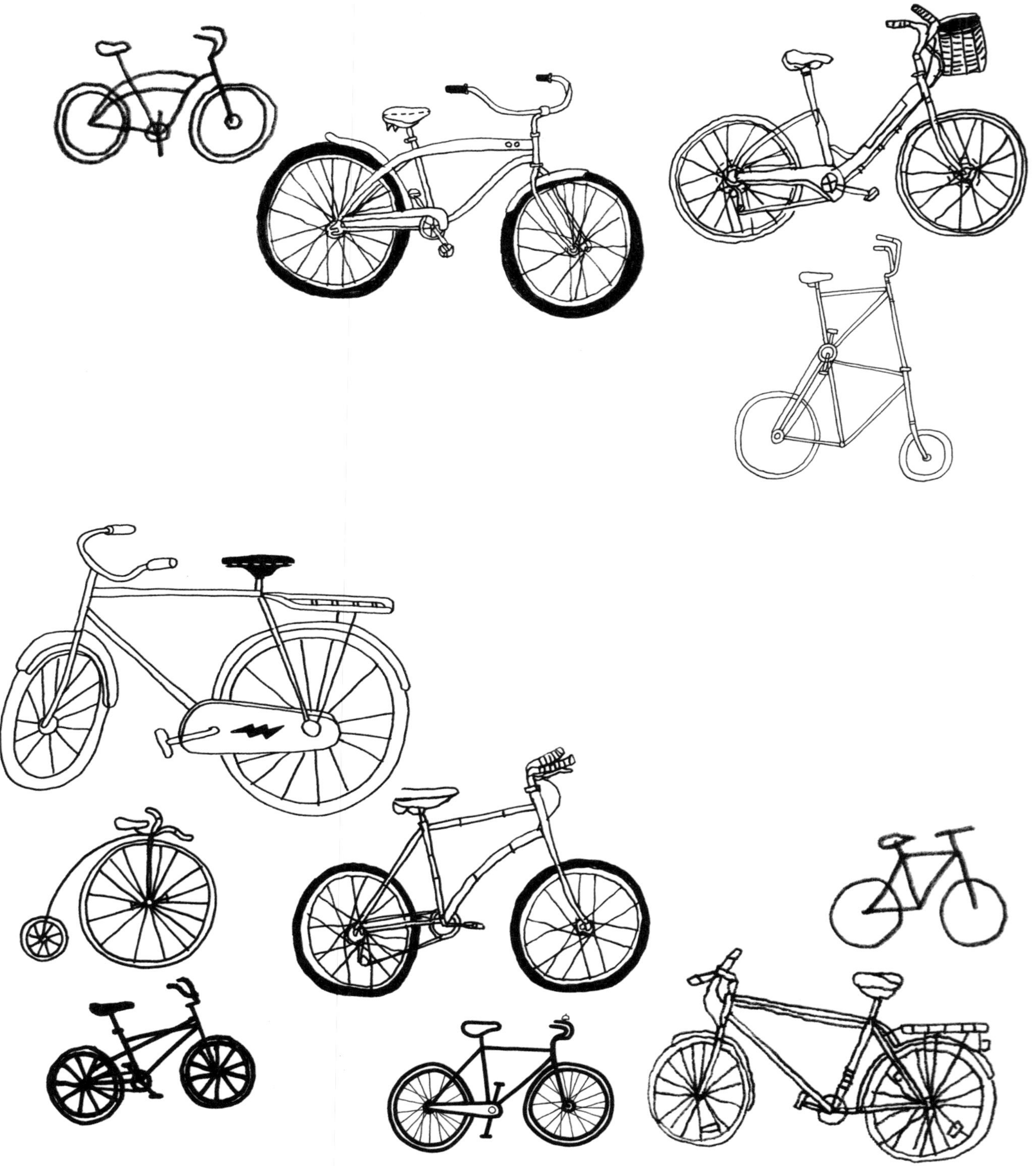

Bikes

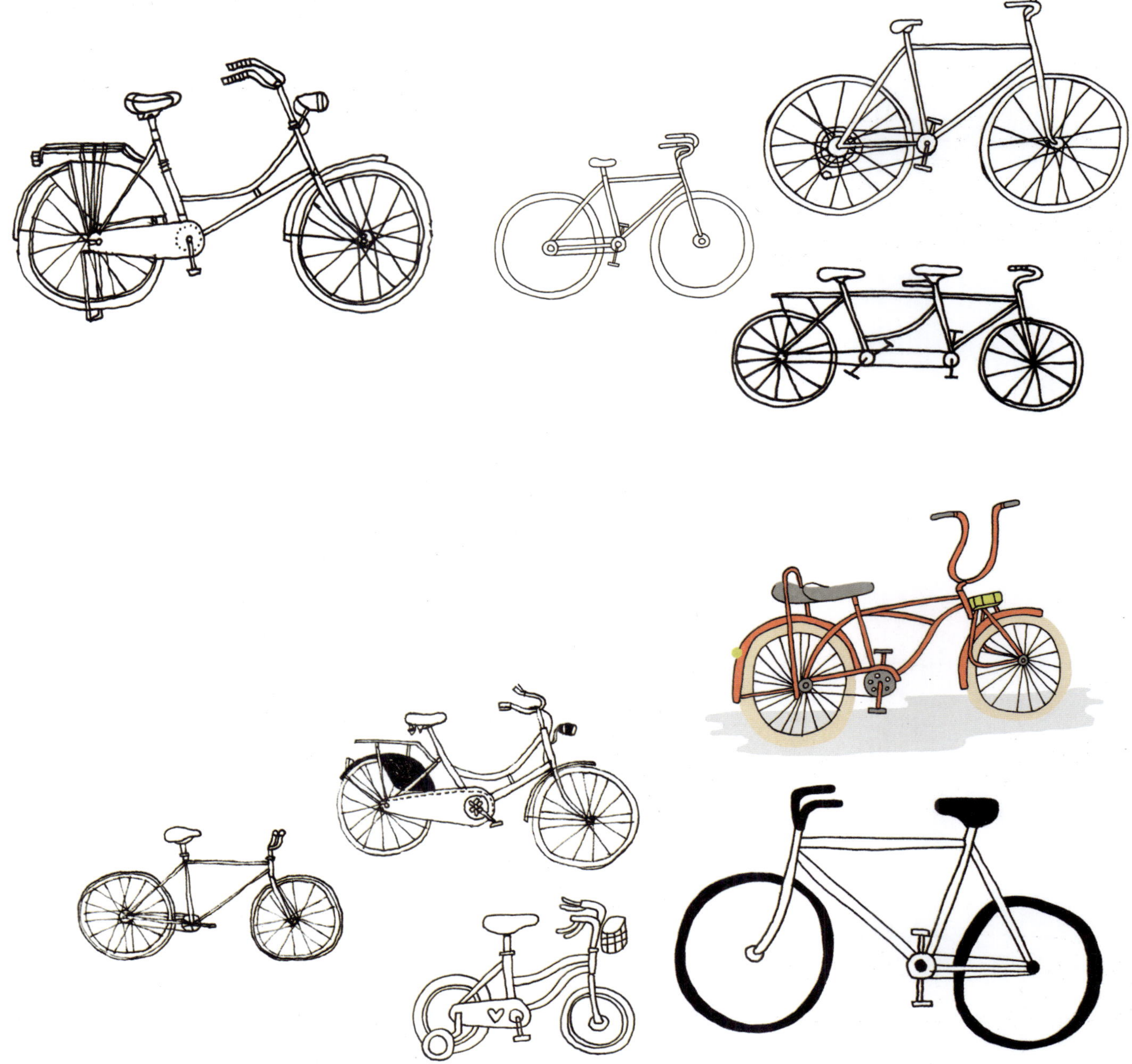

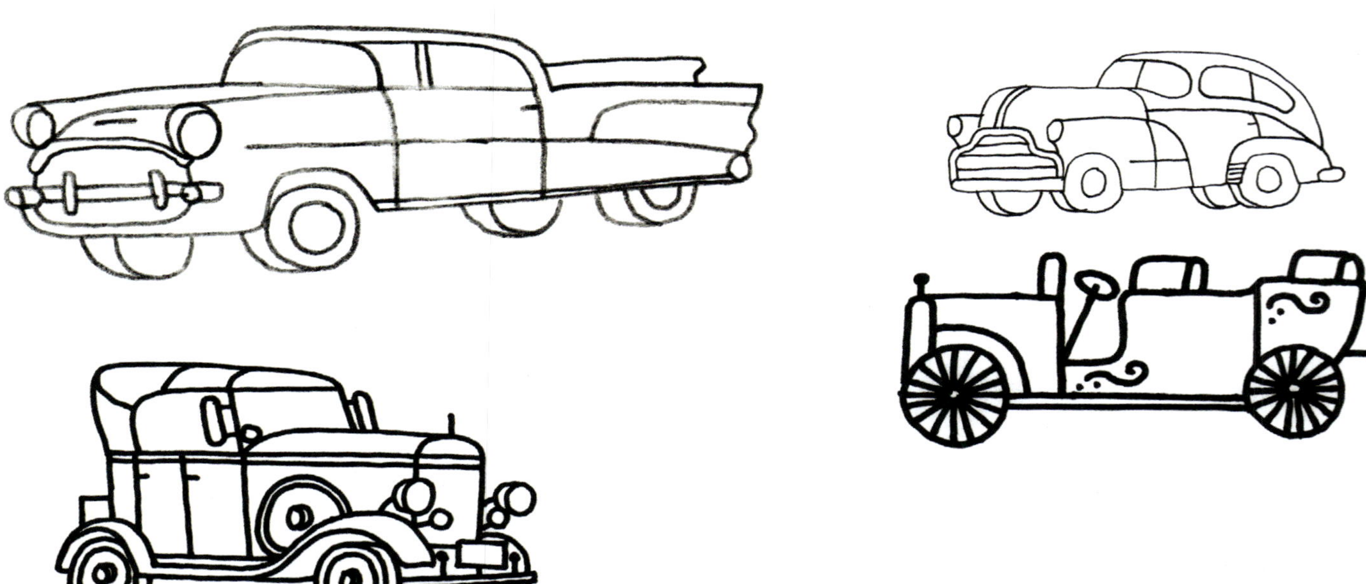

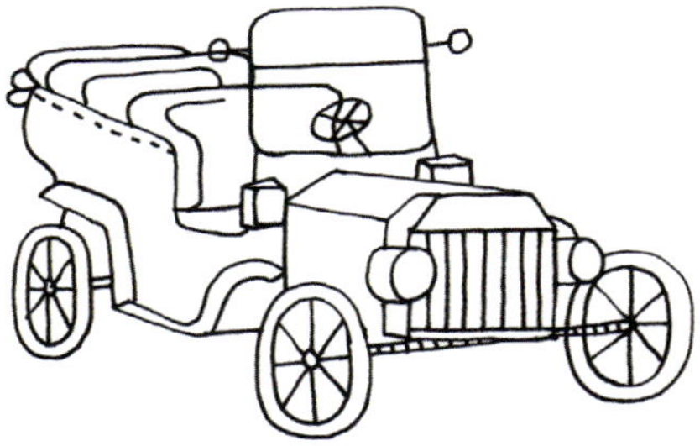

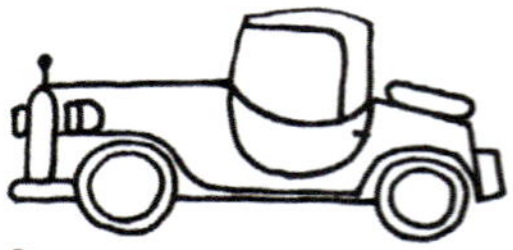

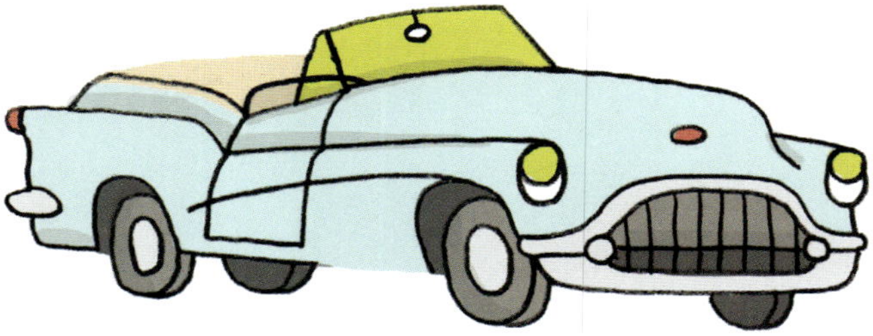

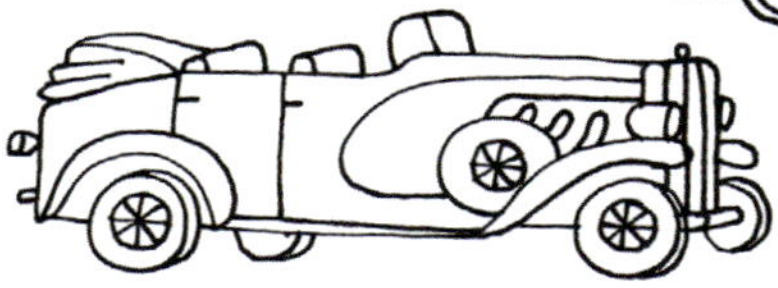

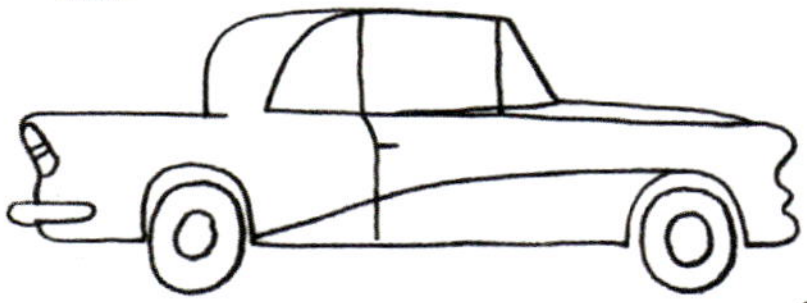

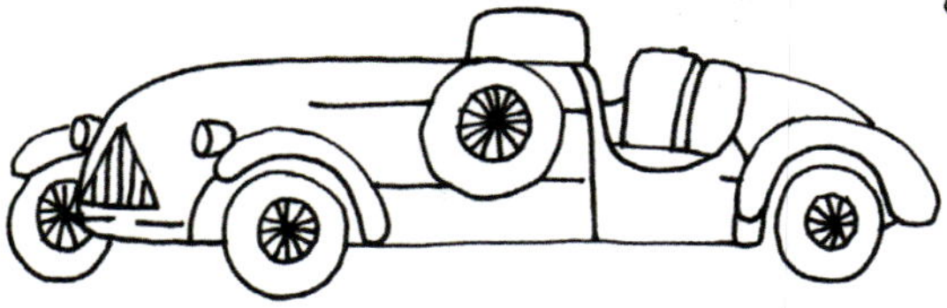

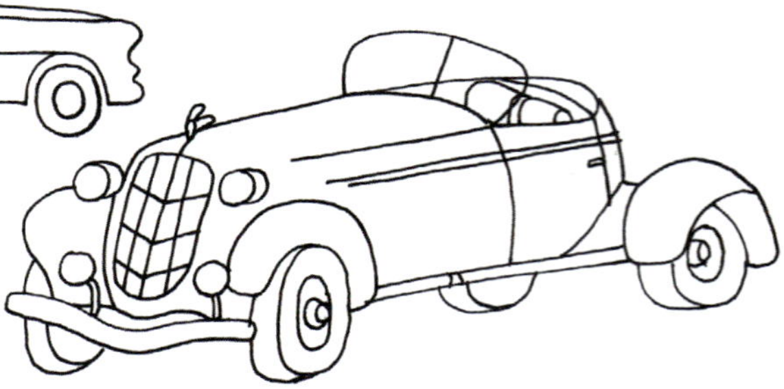

DRAW 20
ANTIQUE AUTOS

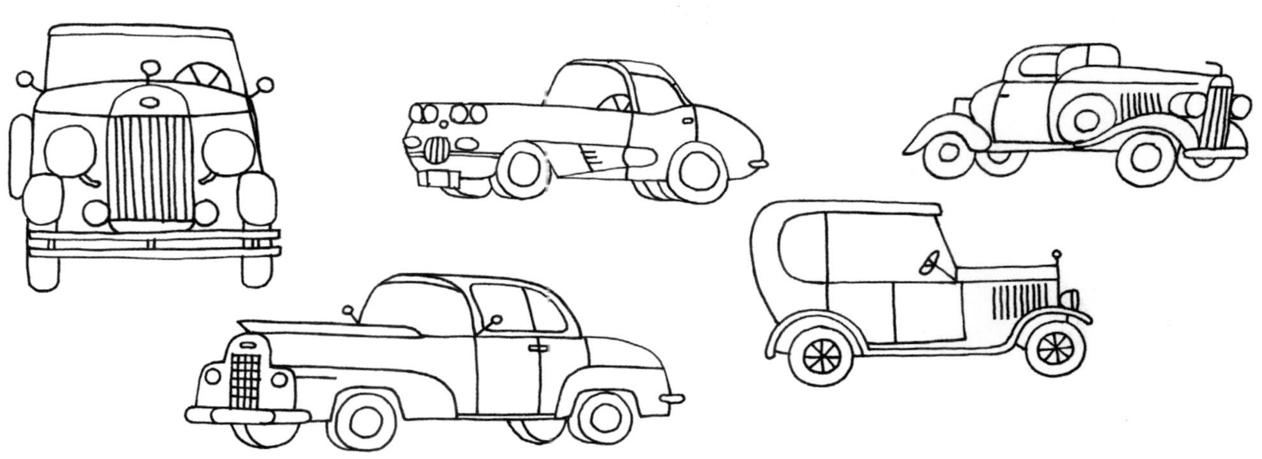

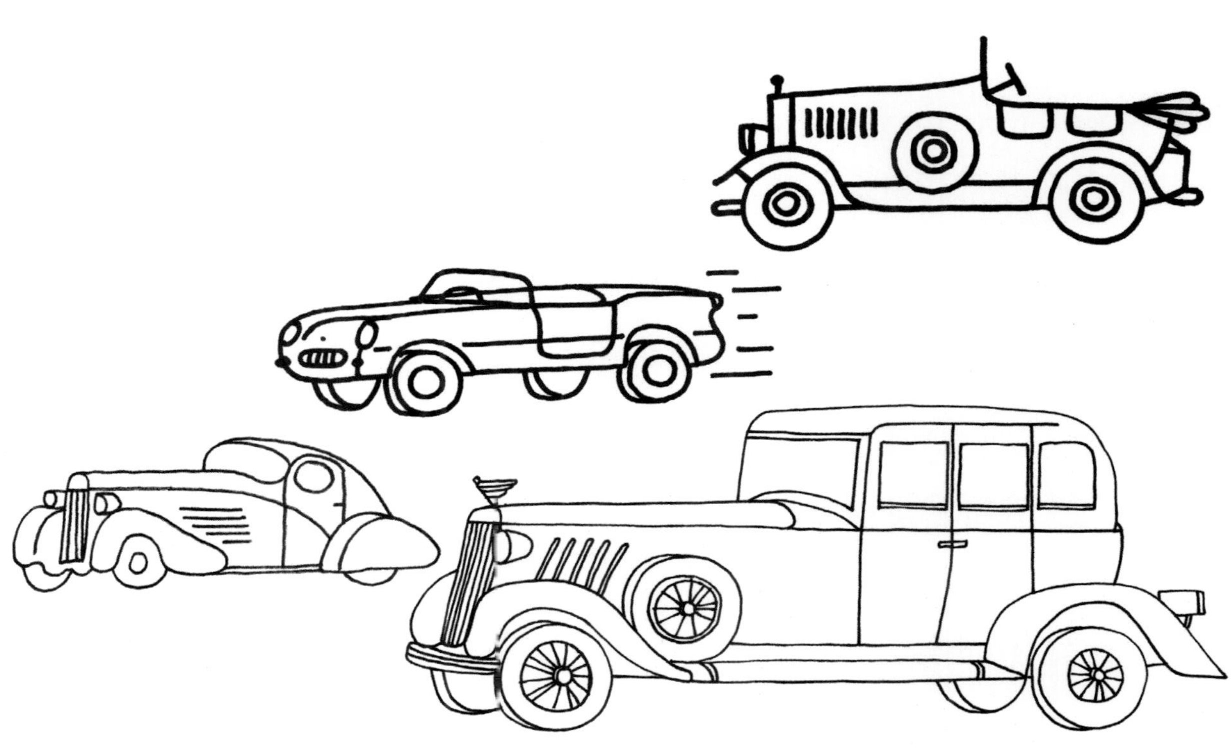

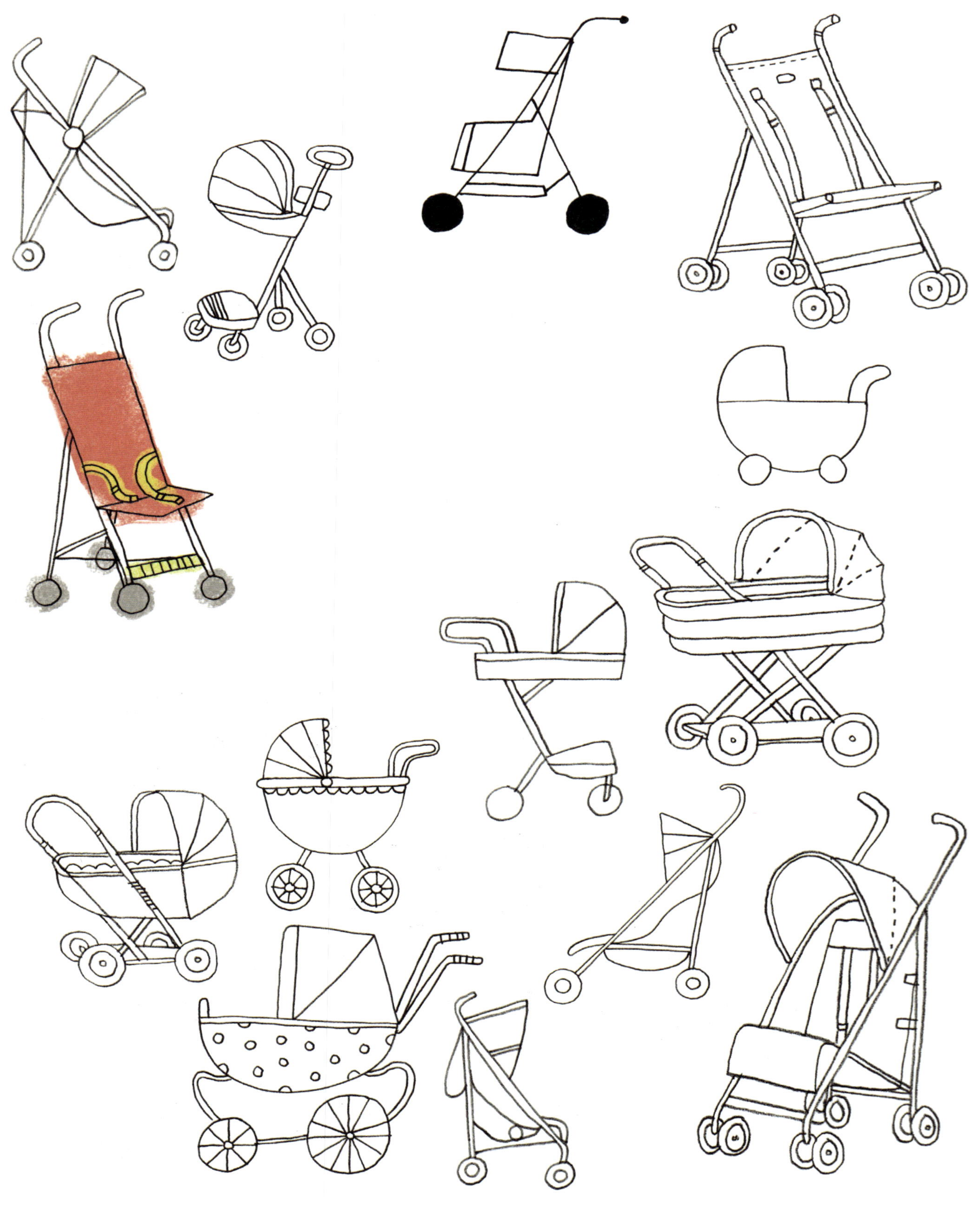

STROLLERS

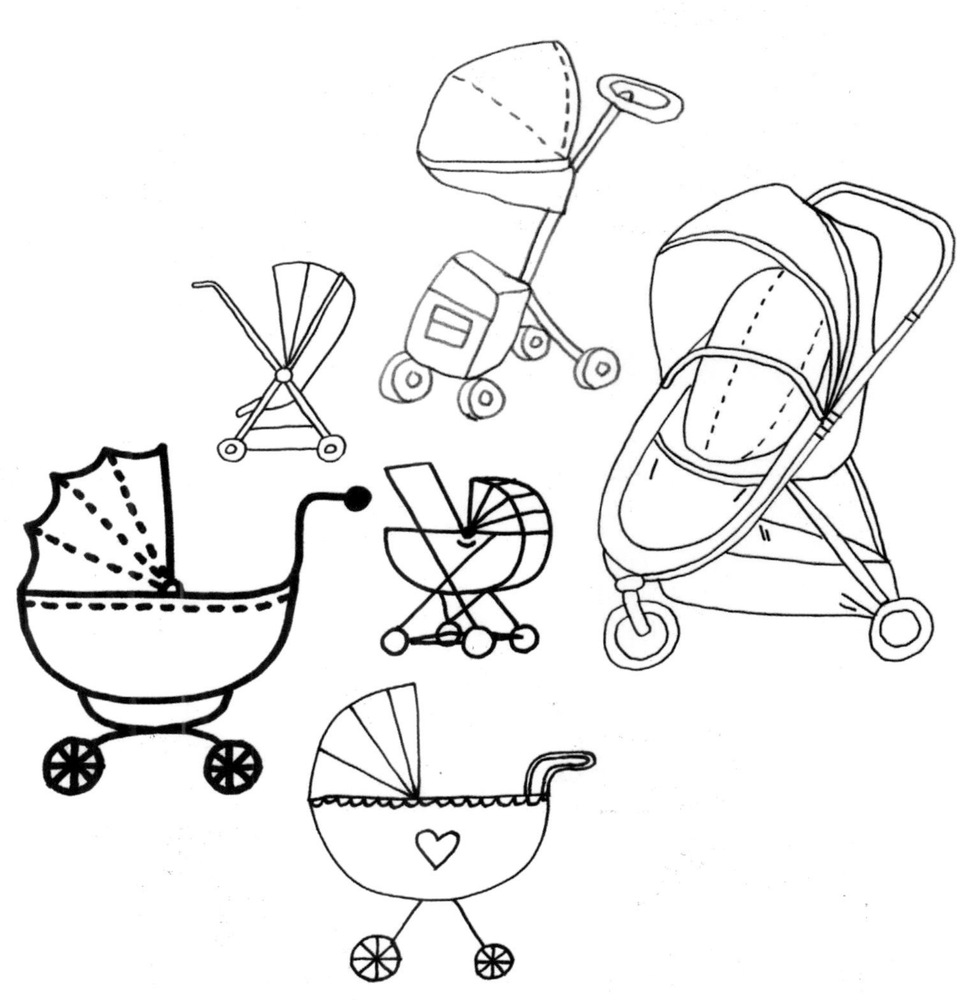

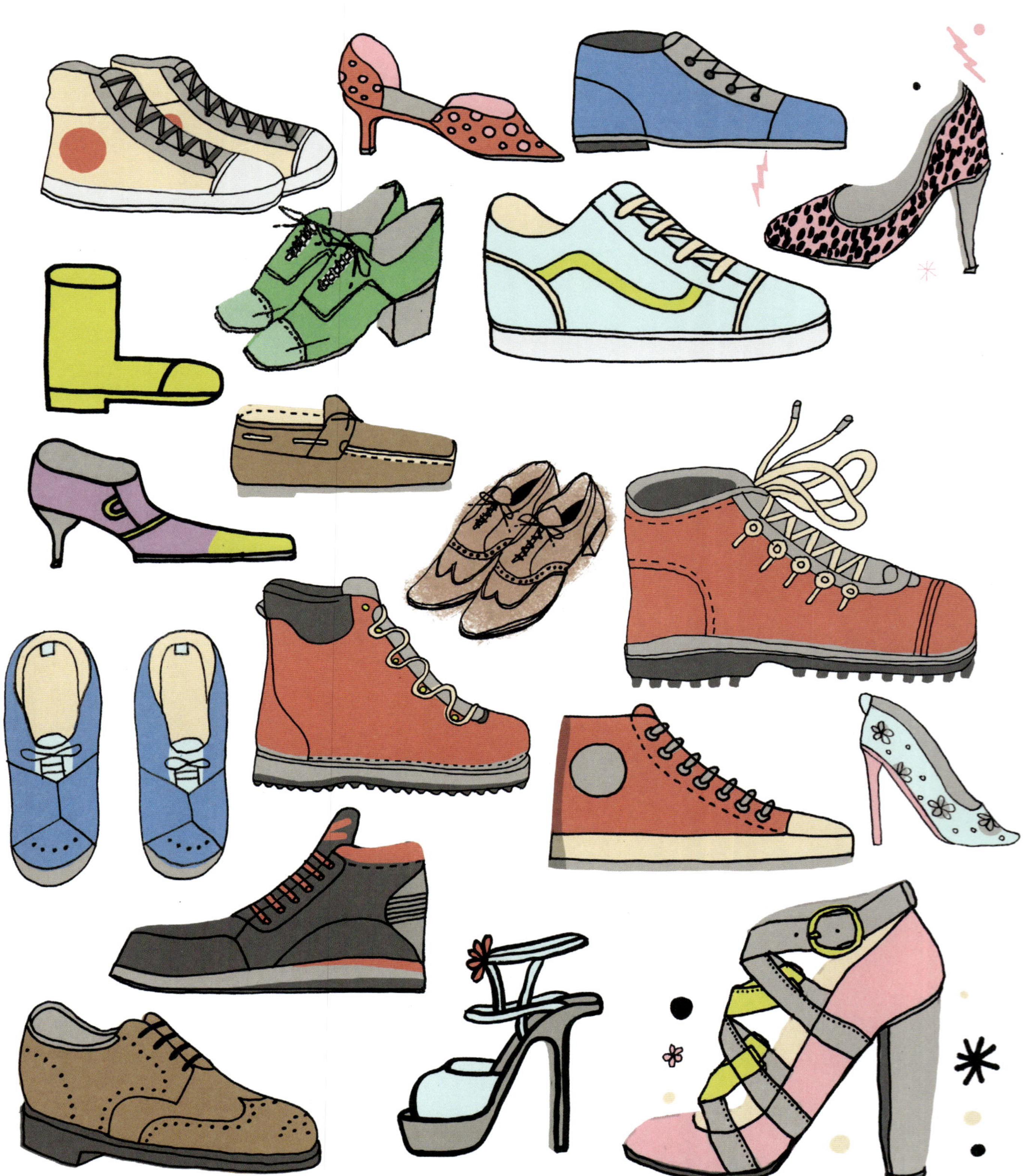

DRAW 20
SHOES

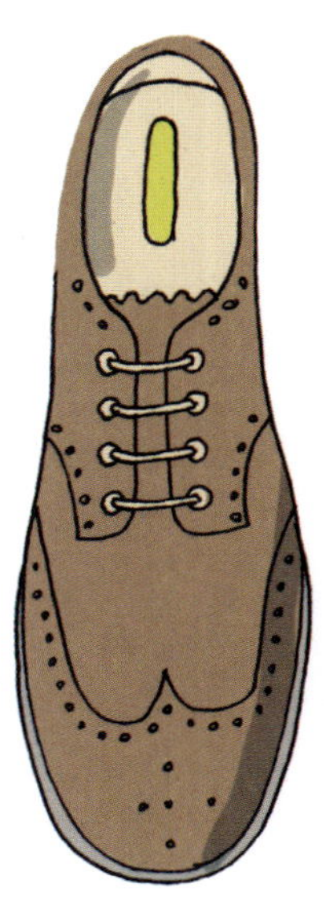

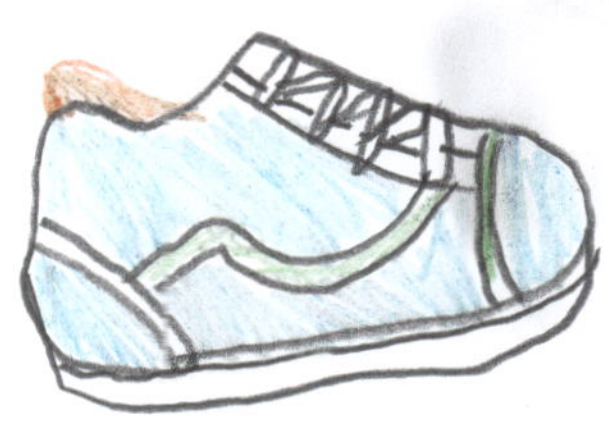

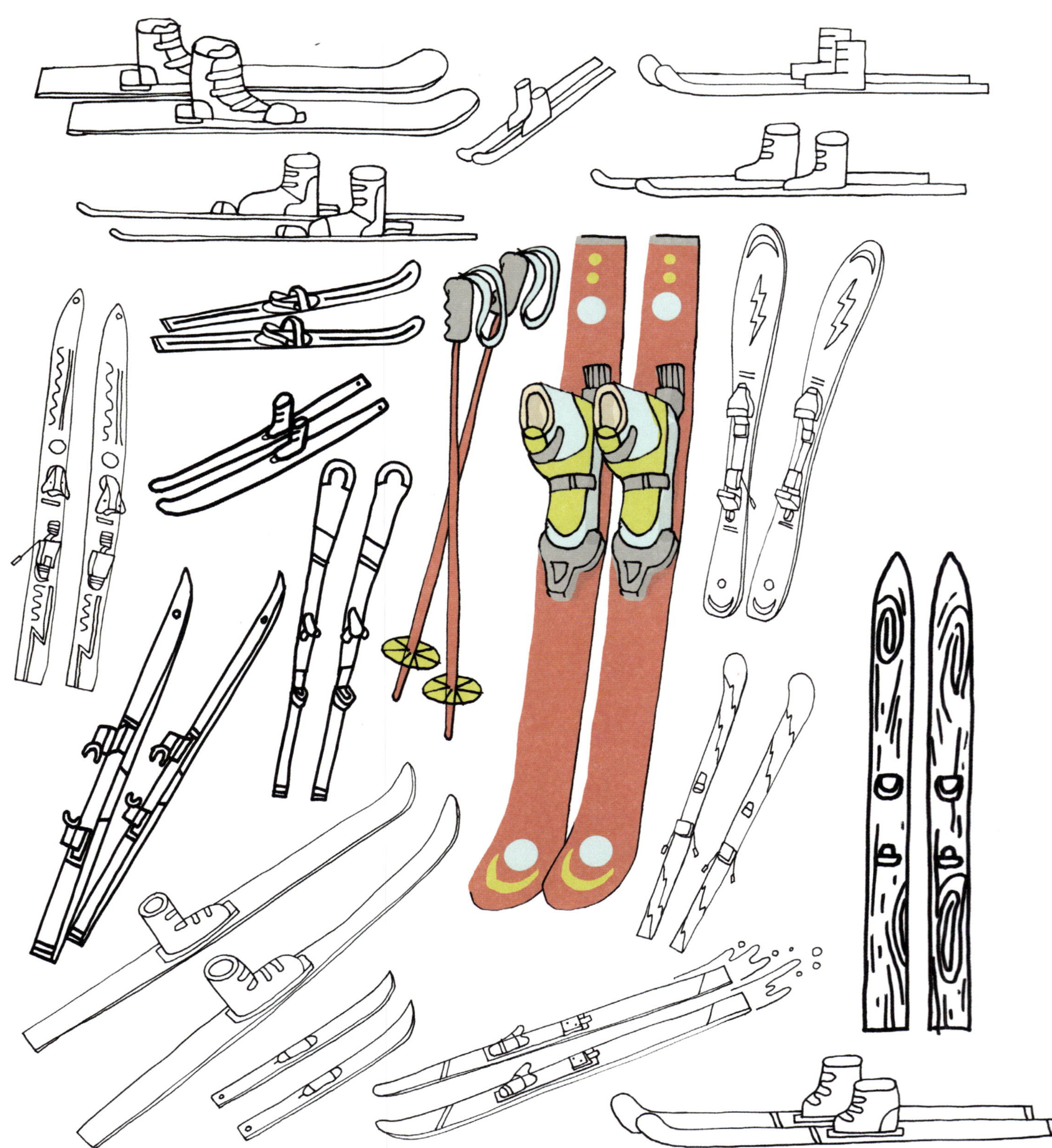

DRAW 20
PAIRS OF SKIS

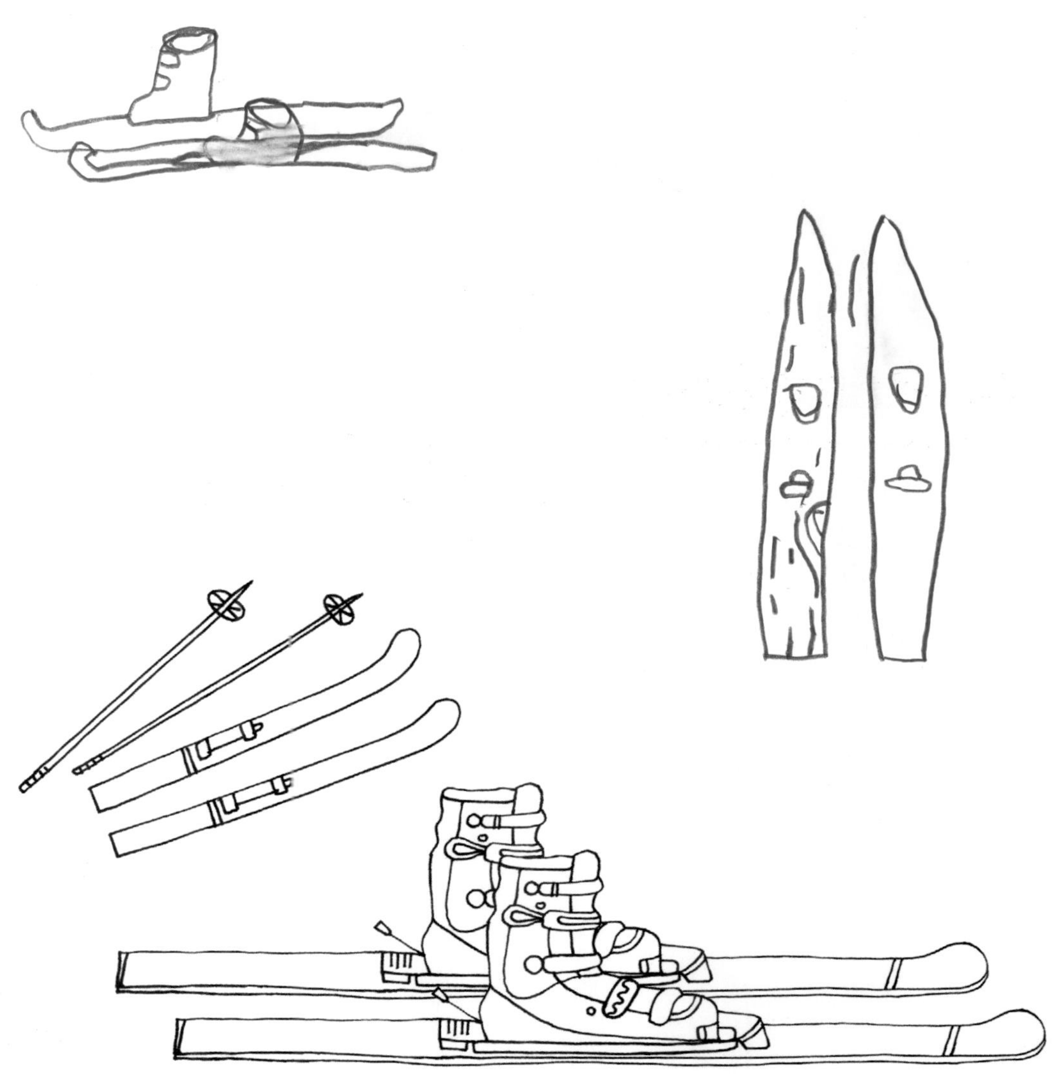

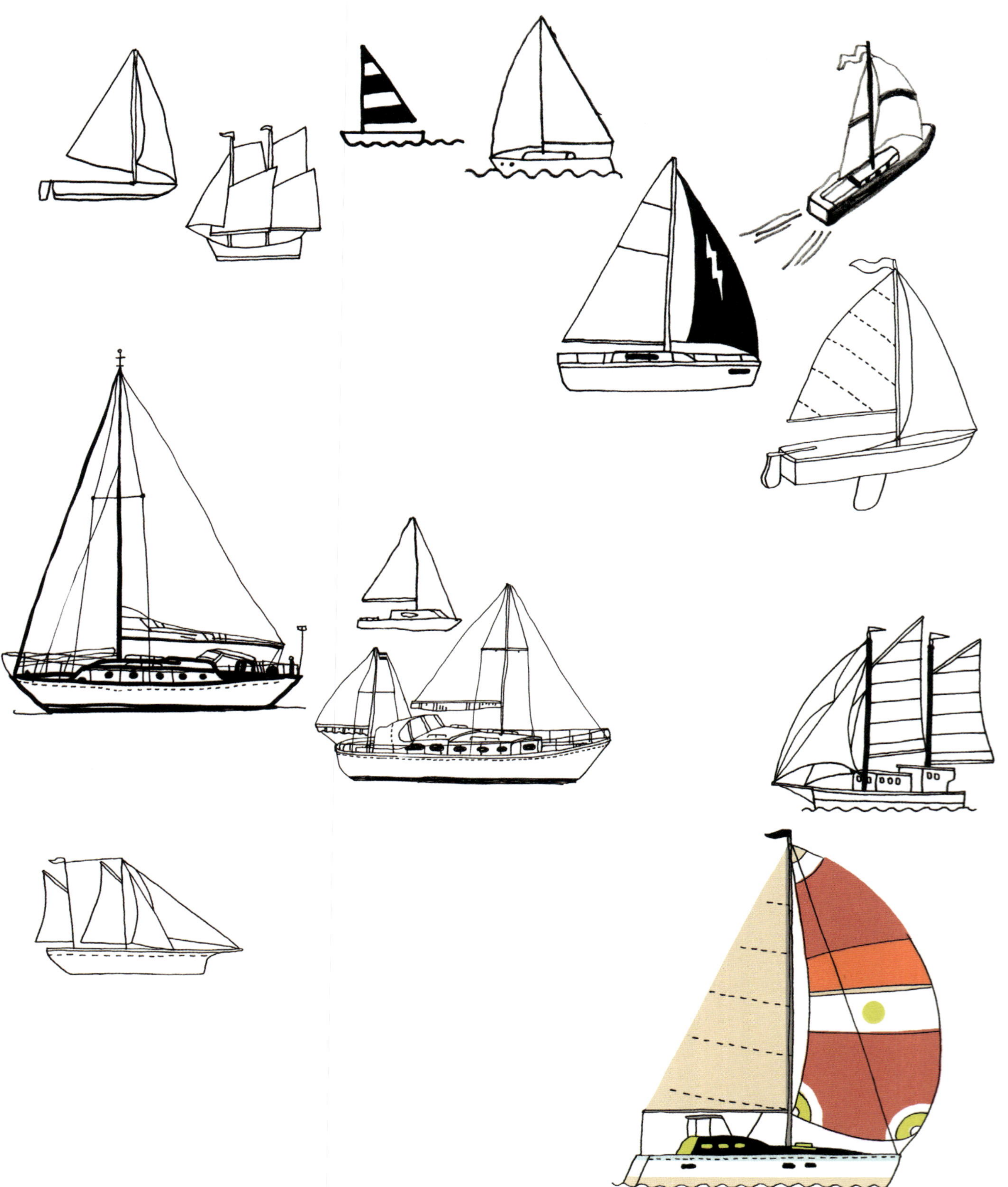

DRAW 20
Sailboats

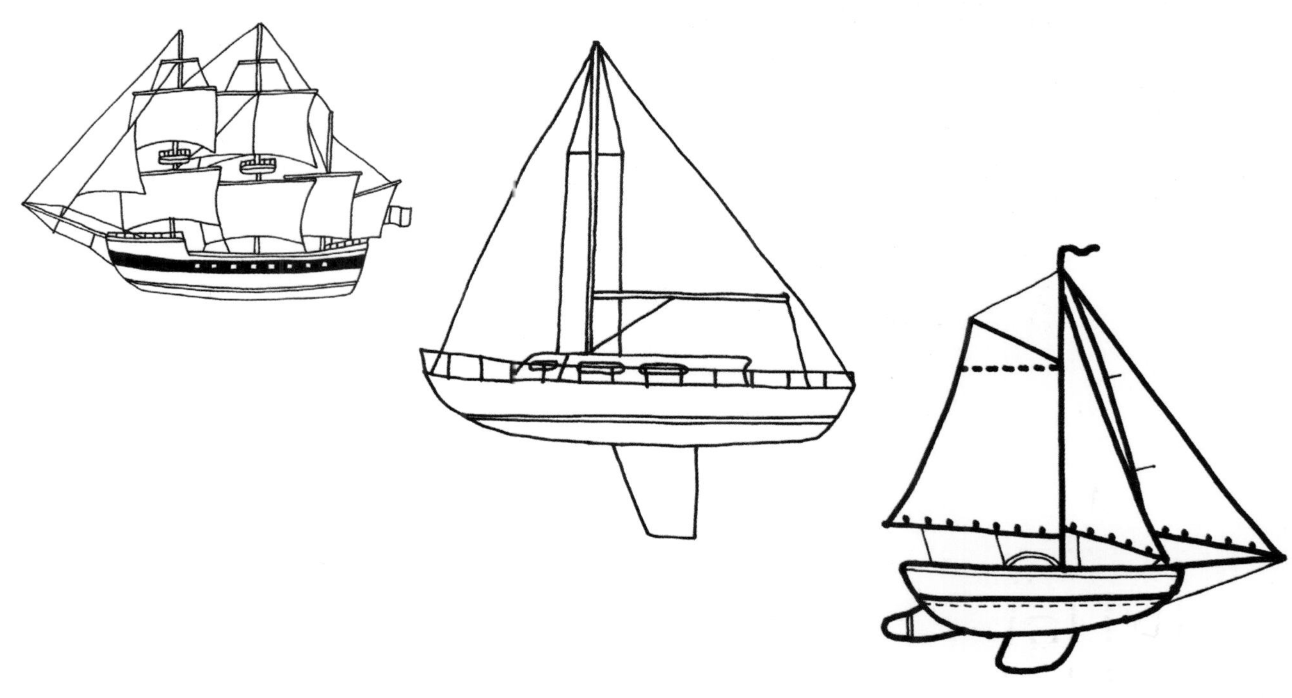

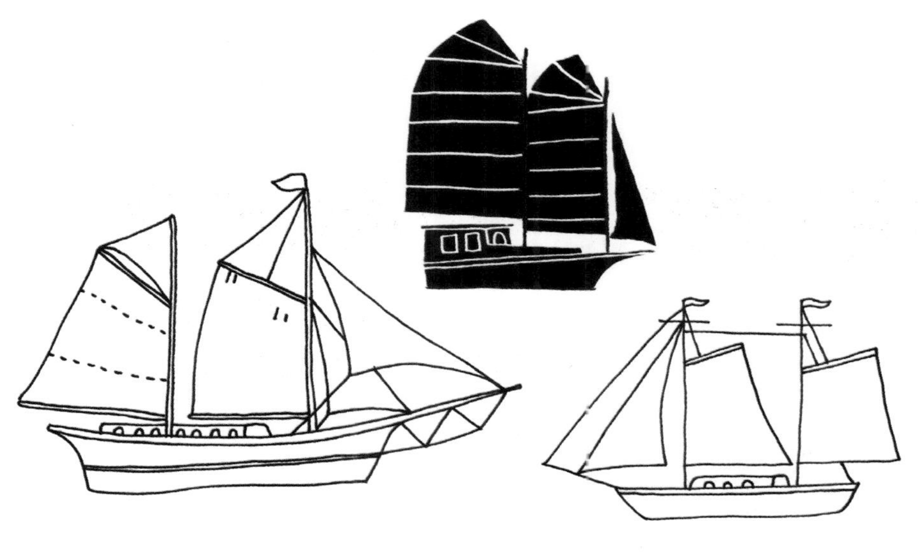

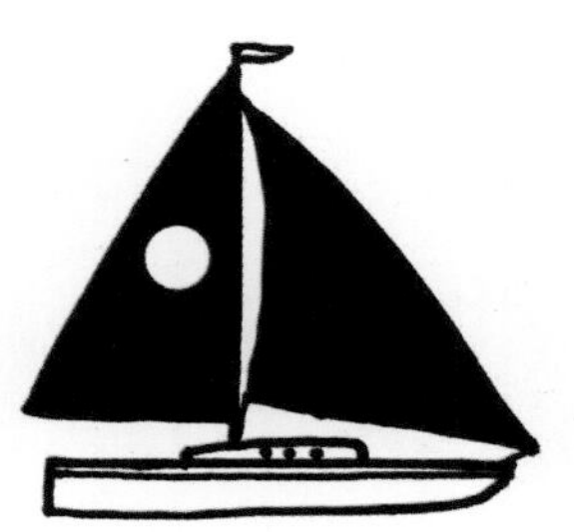

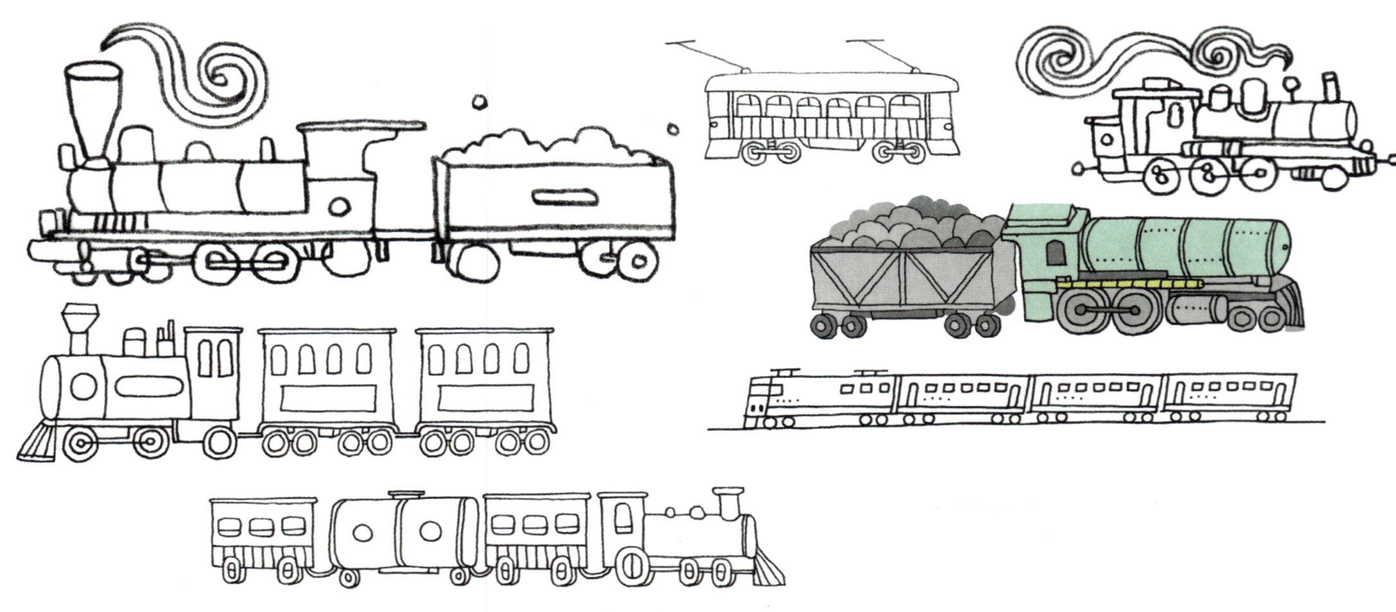

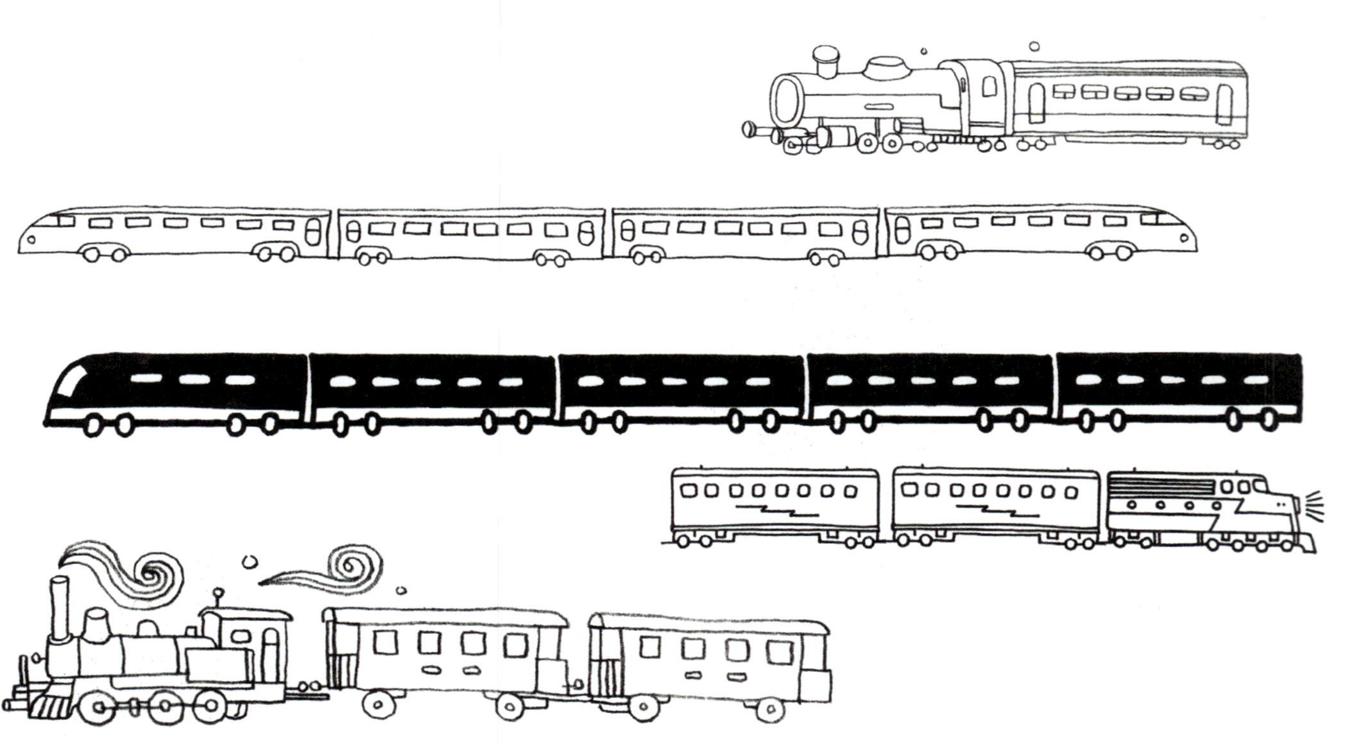

DRAW 20
TRAINS

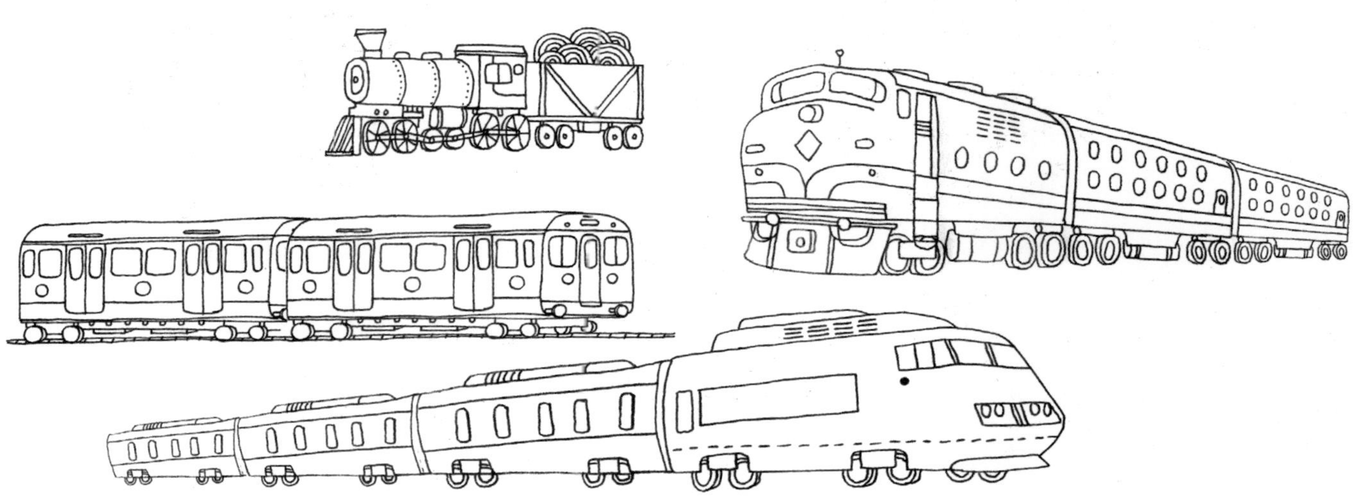

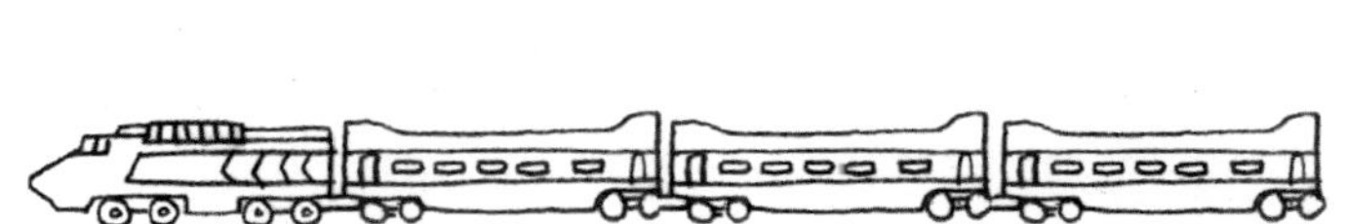

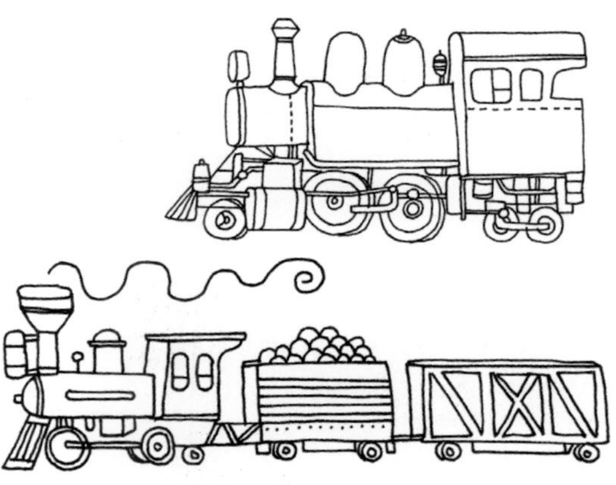

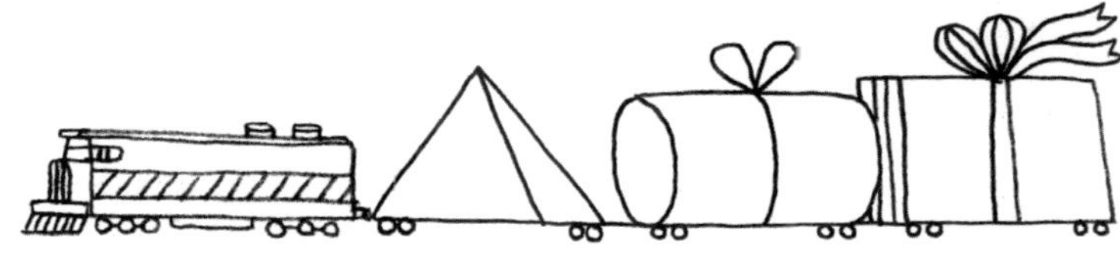

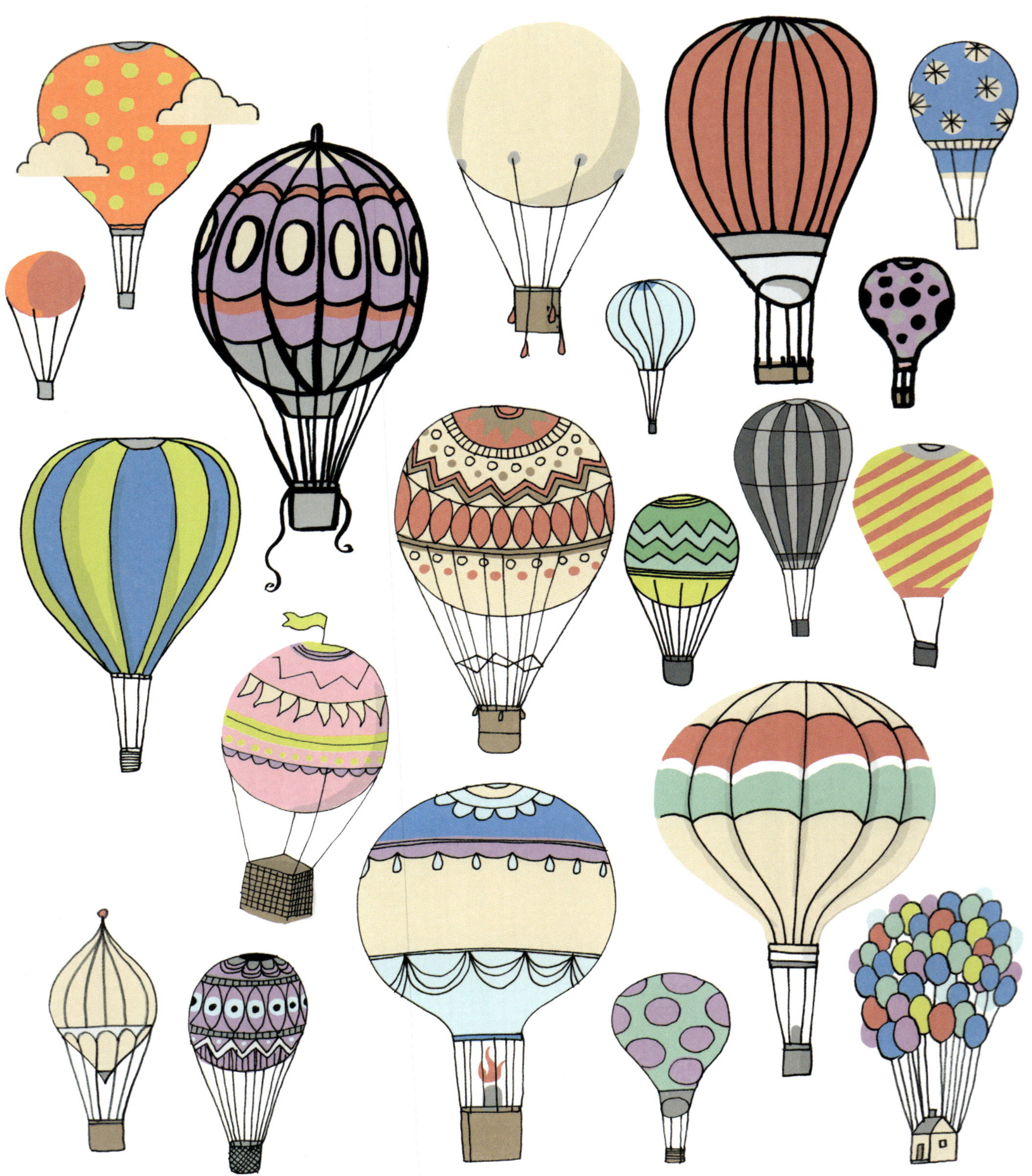

DRAW 20
HOT-AIR BALLOONS

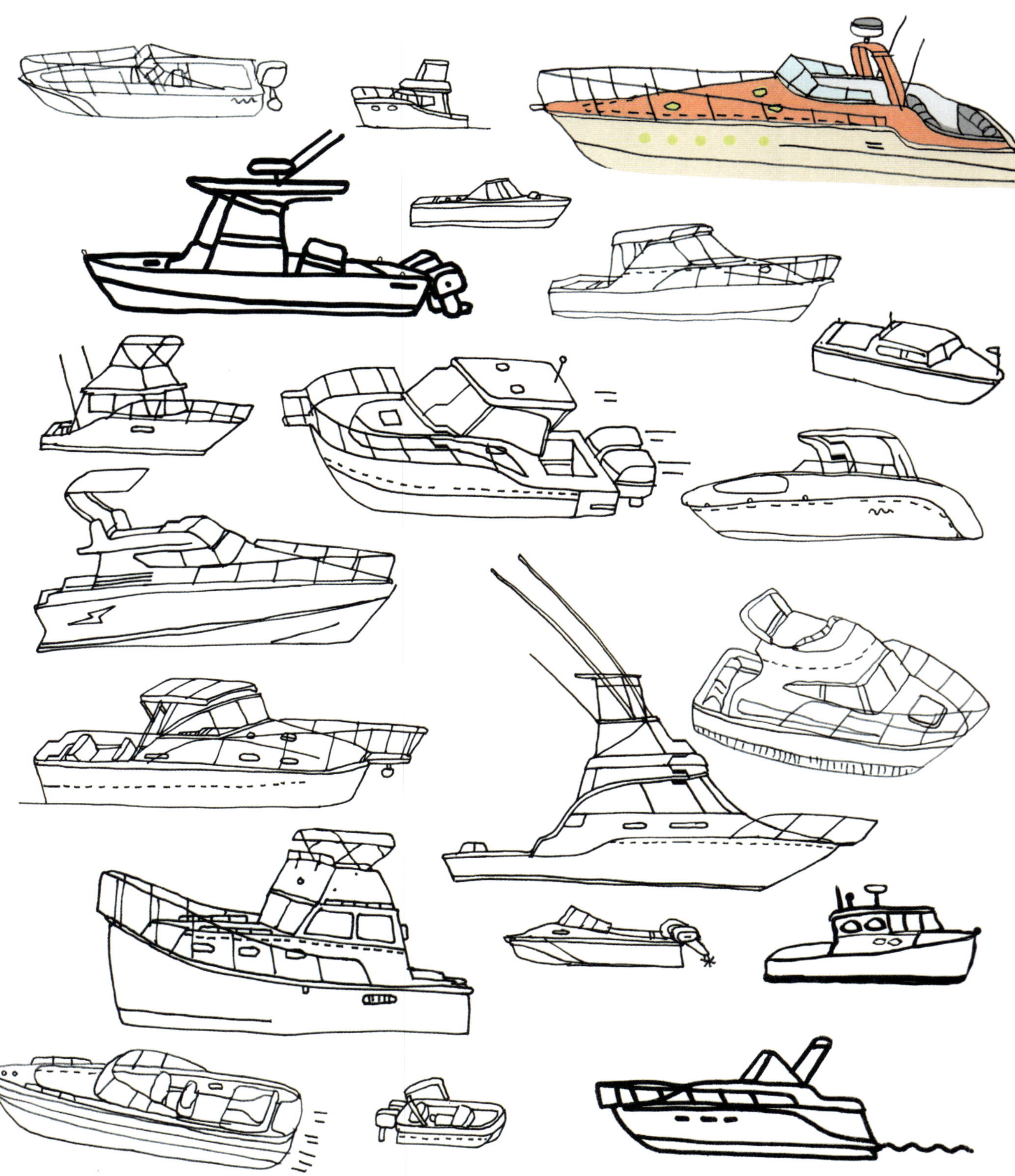

DRAW 20
MOTORBOATS

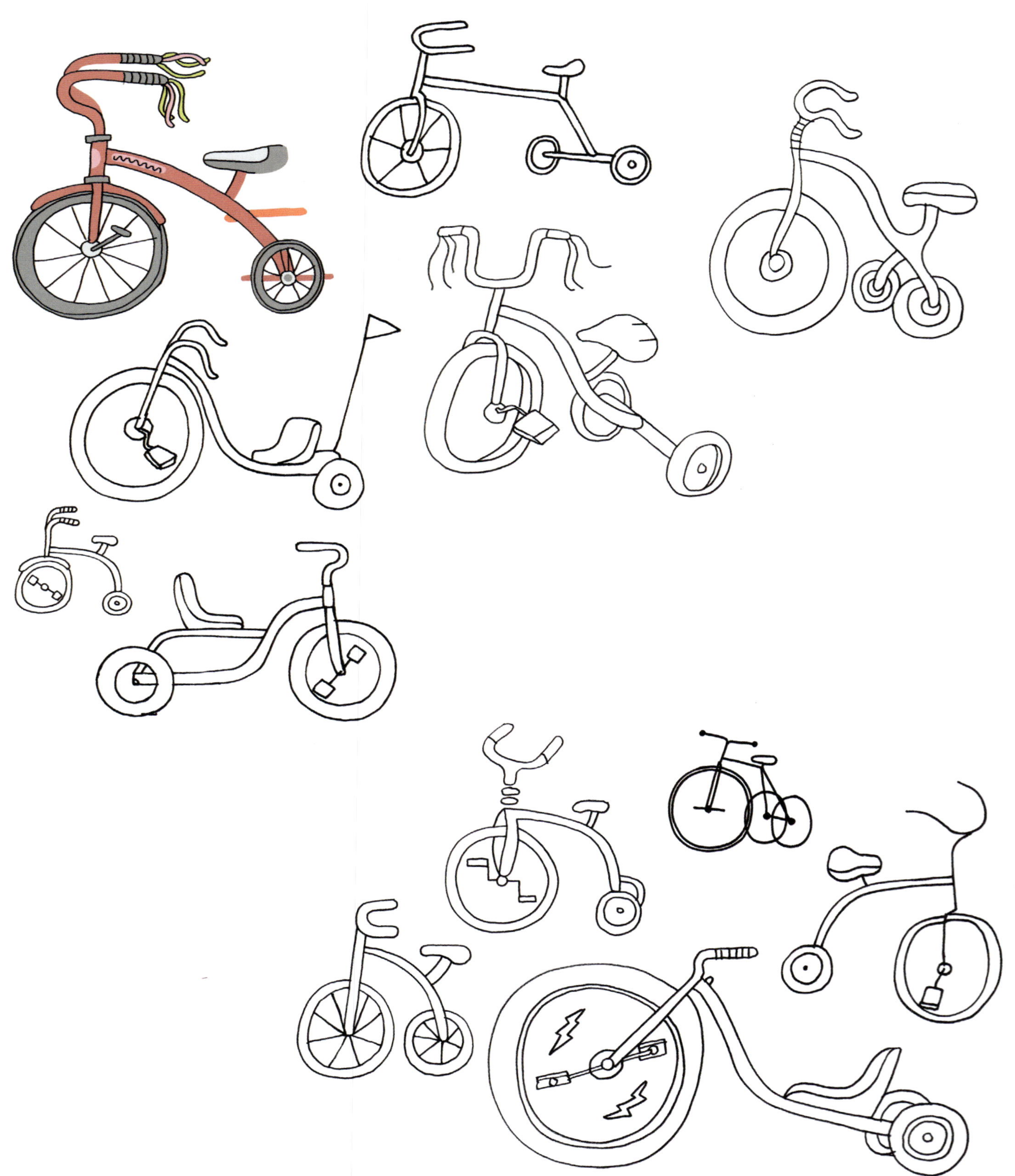

TRICYCLES

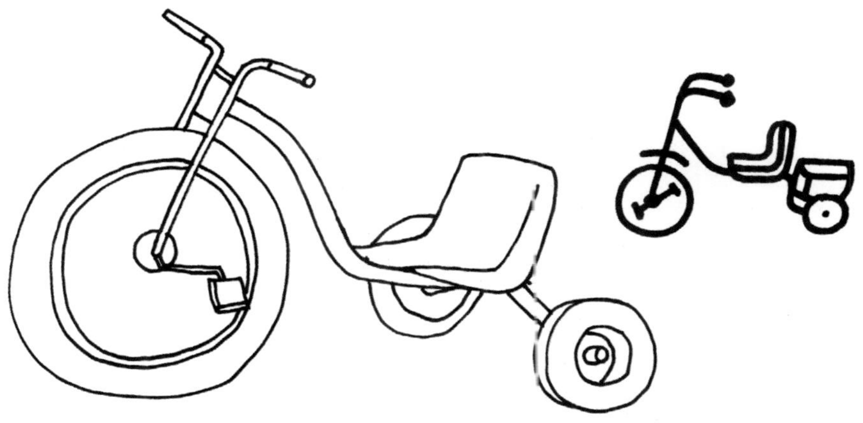

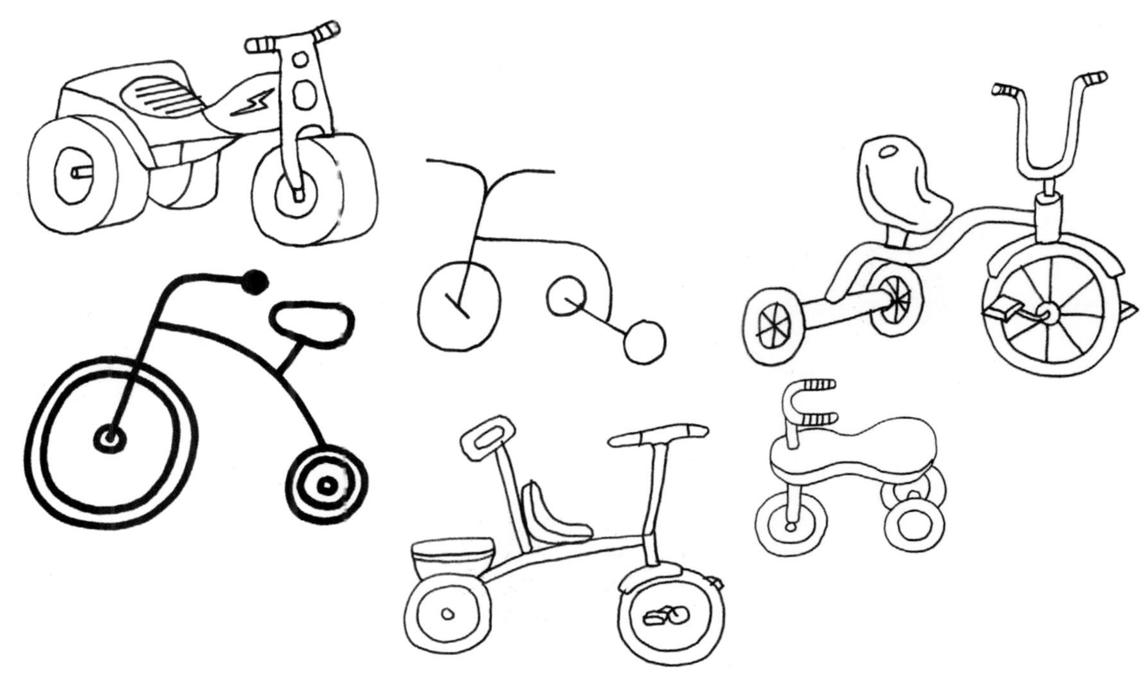

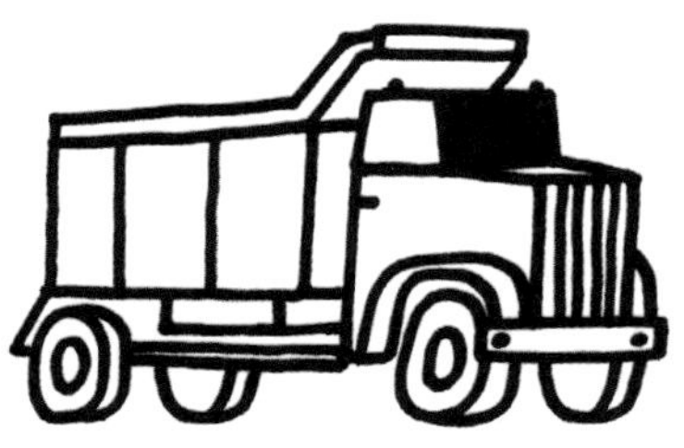
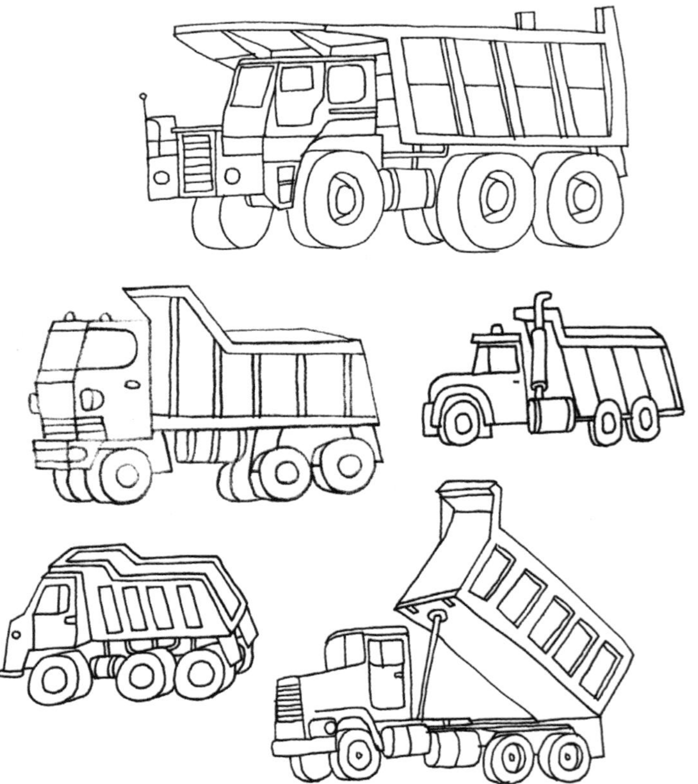
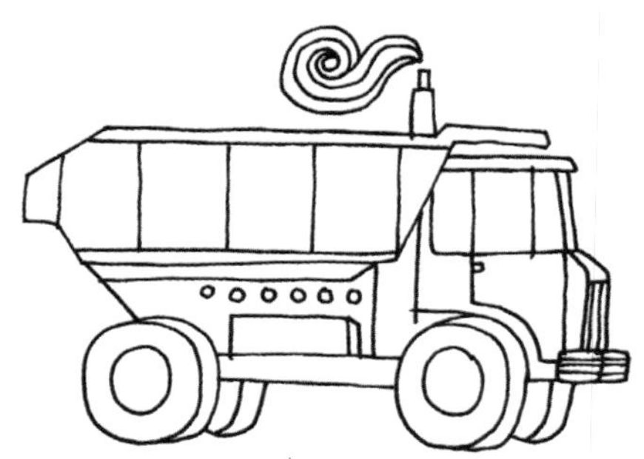
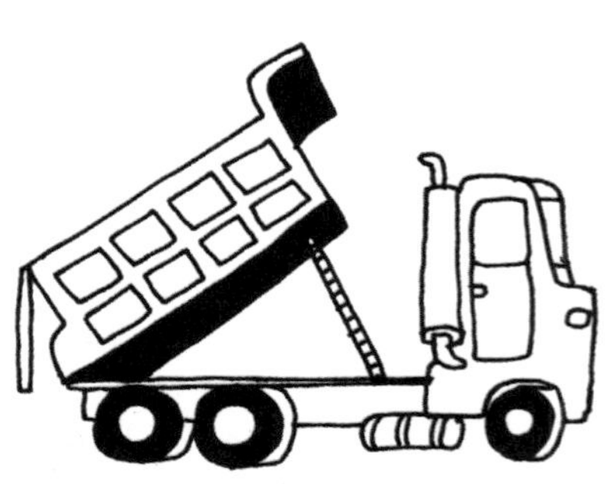
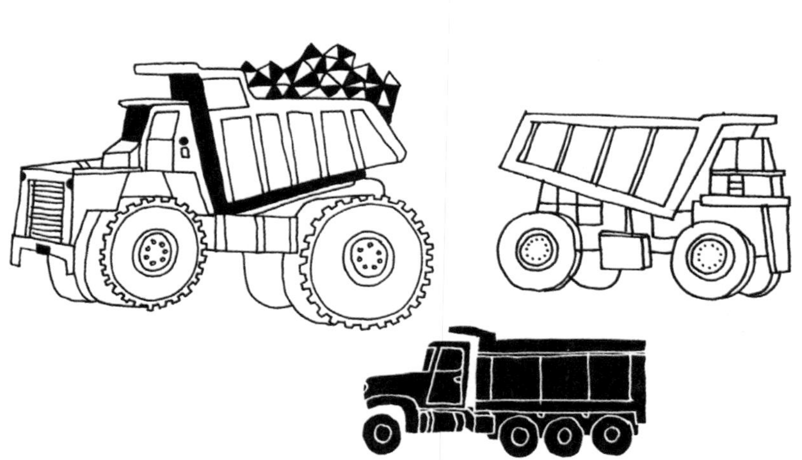
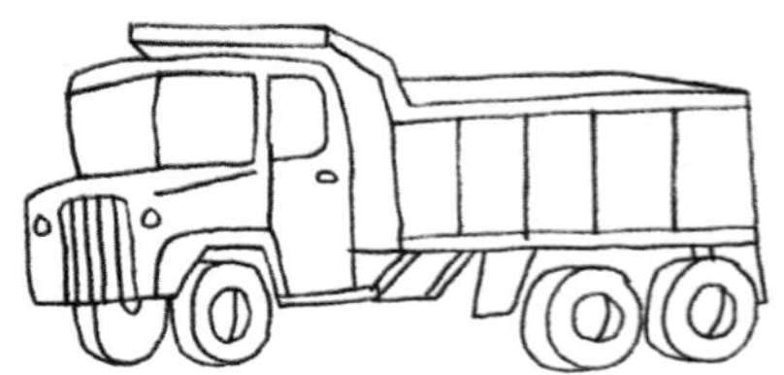

DRAW 20
DUMP TRUCKS

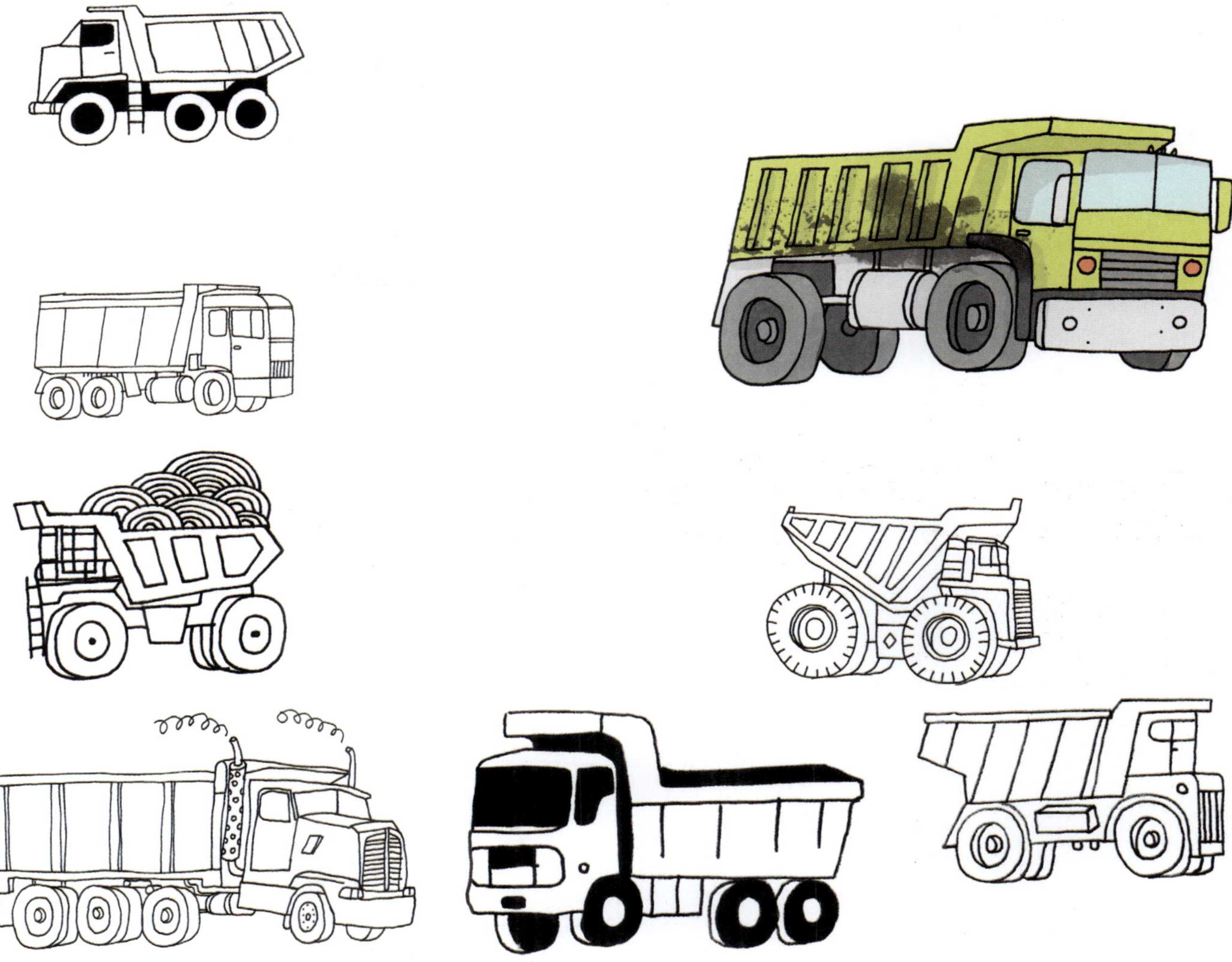

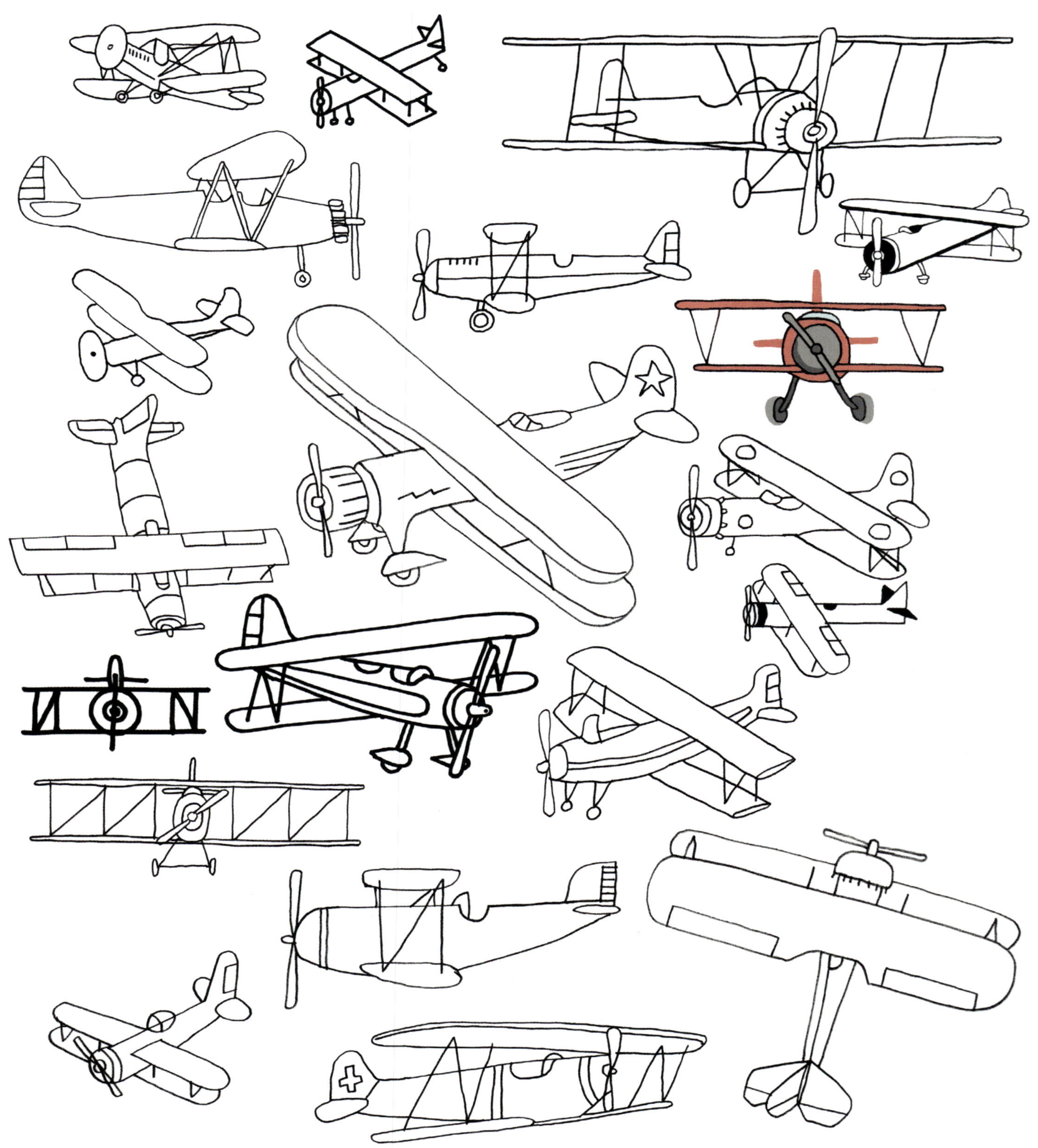

DRAW 20
BIPLANES

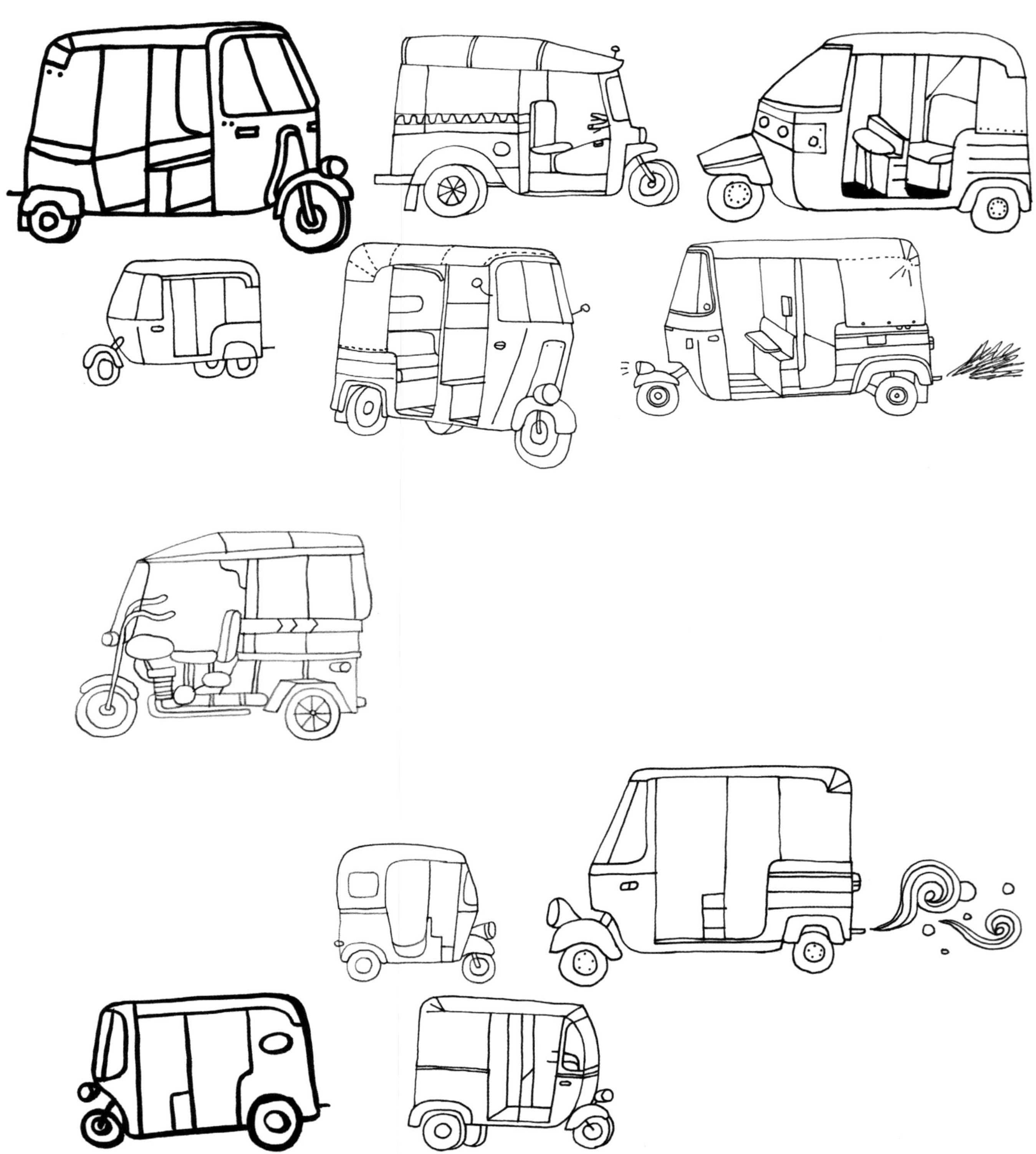

DRAW 20

RICKSHAWS

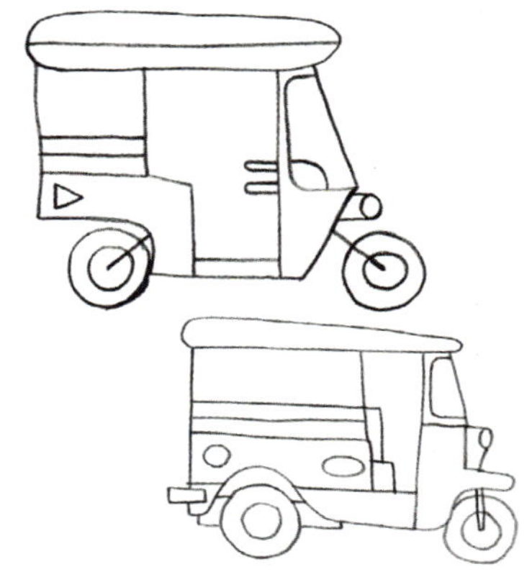

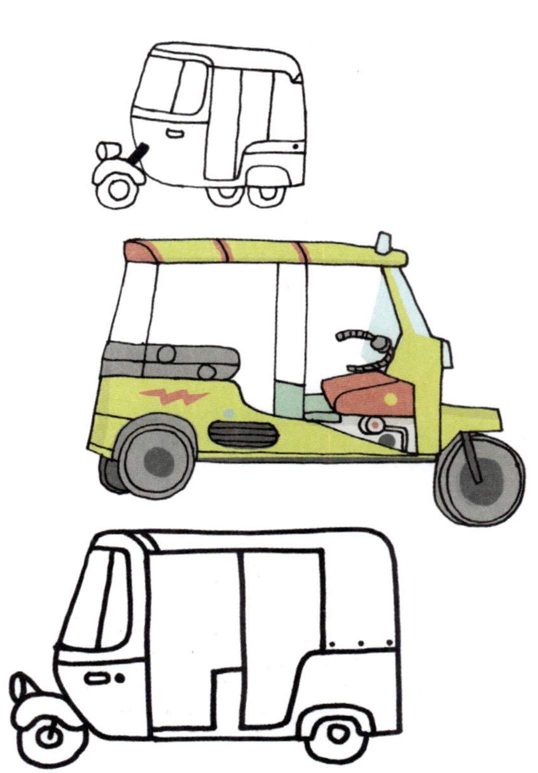

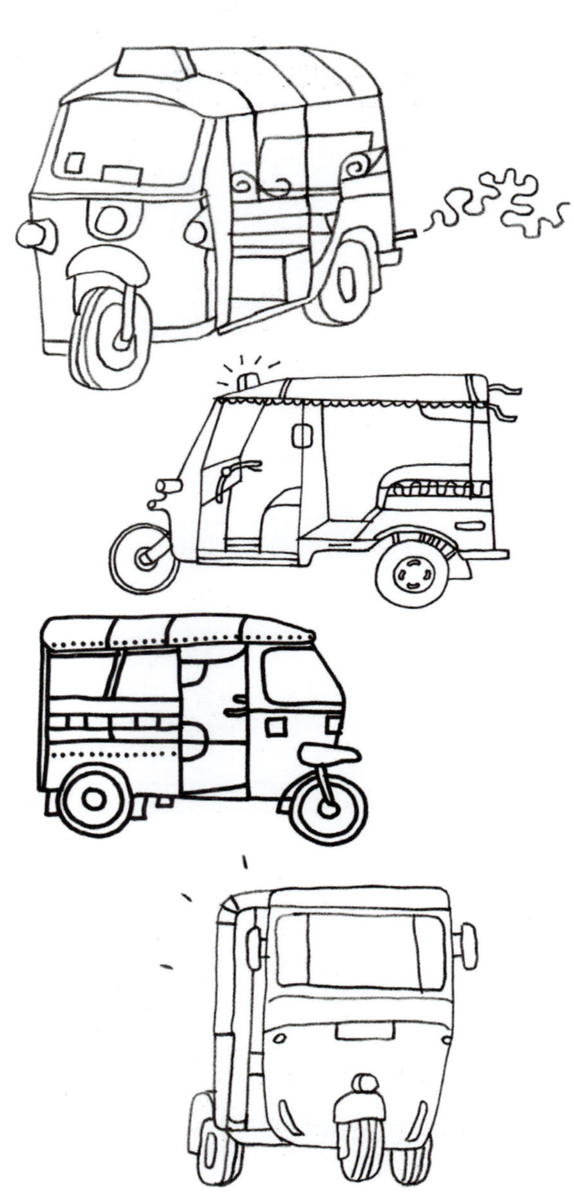

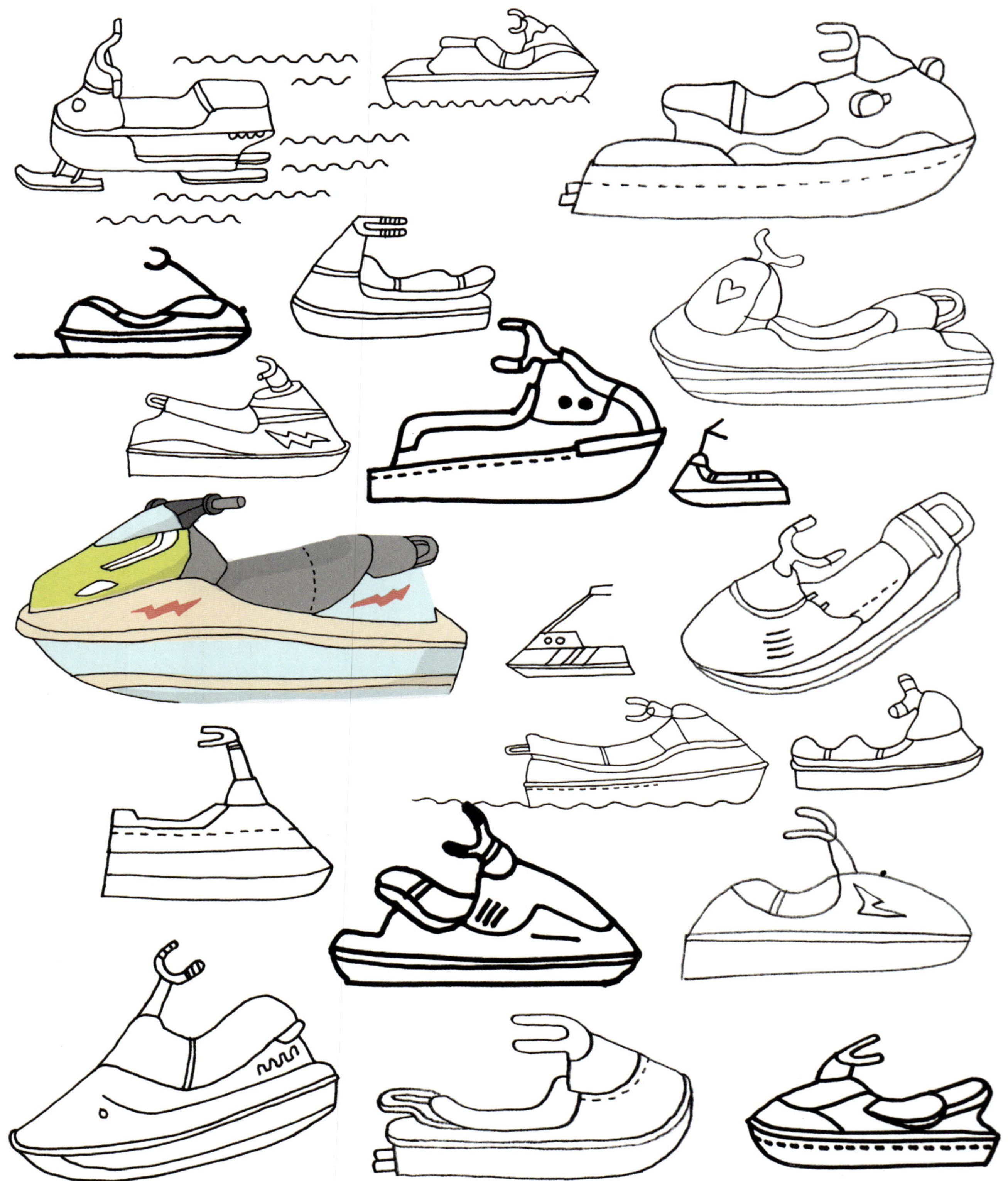

DRAW 20
JET SKIS

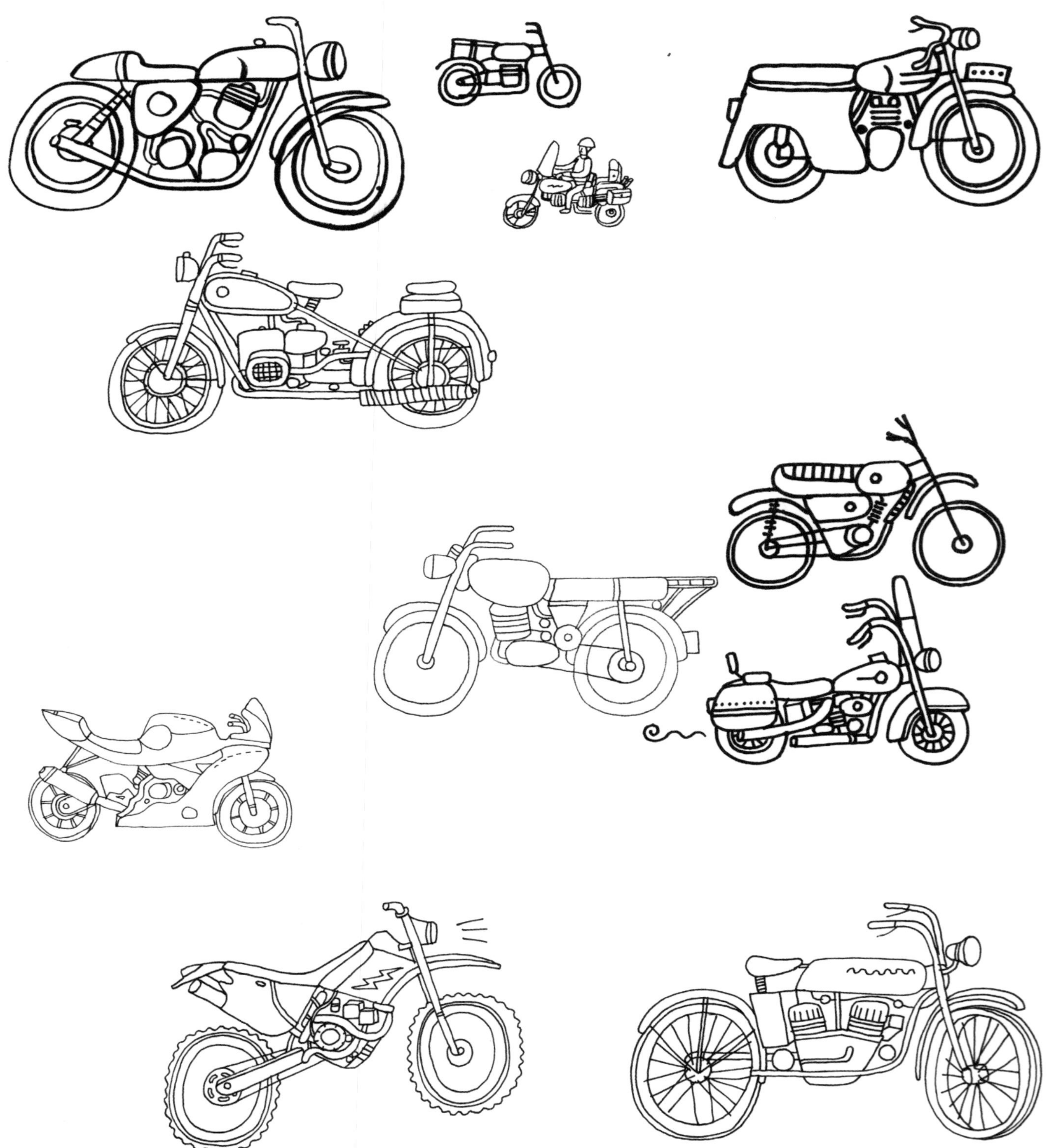

Motorcycles

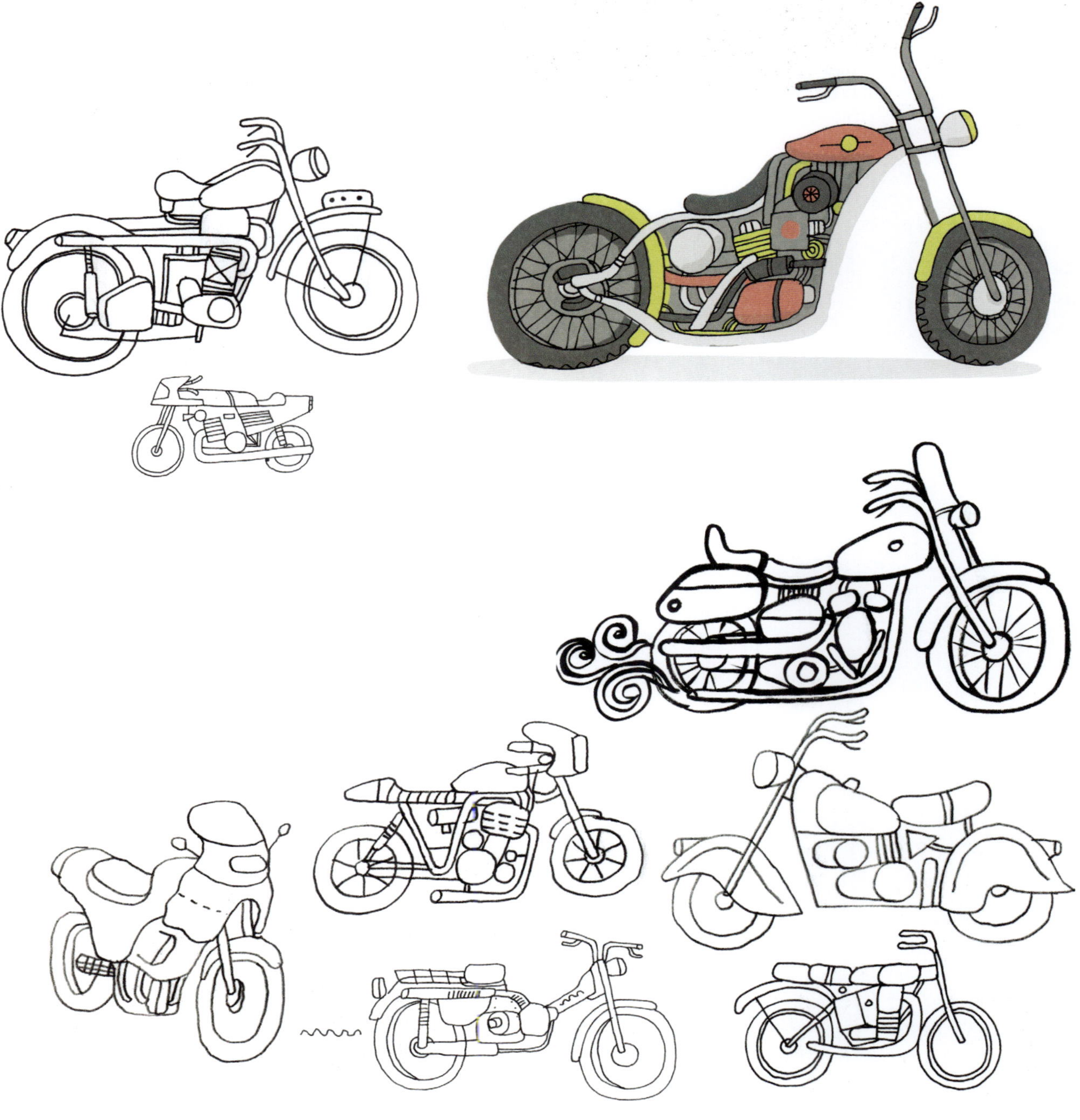

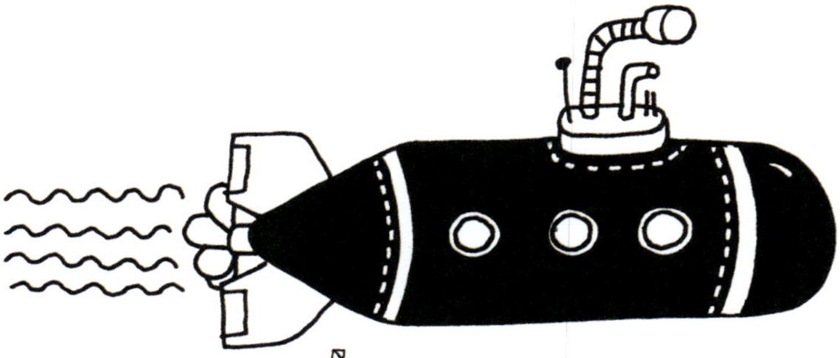

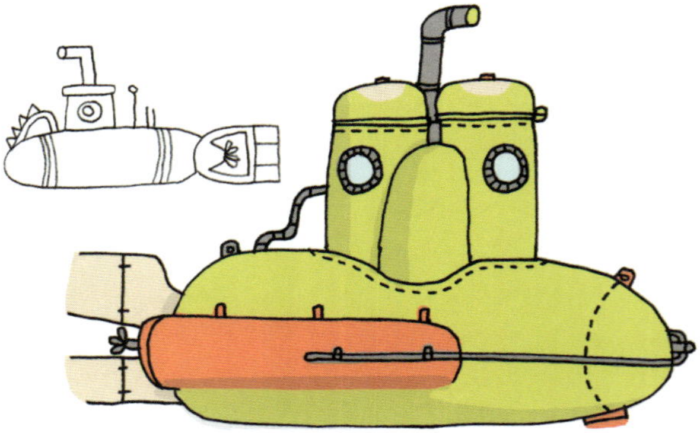

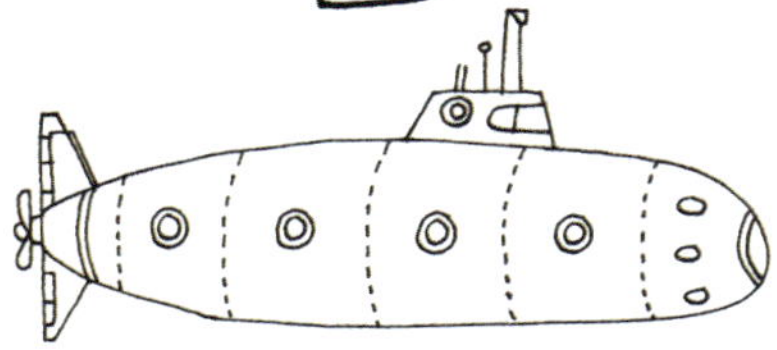

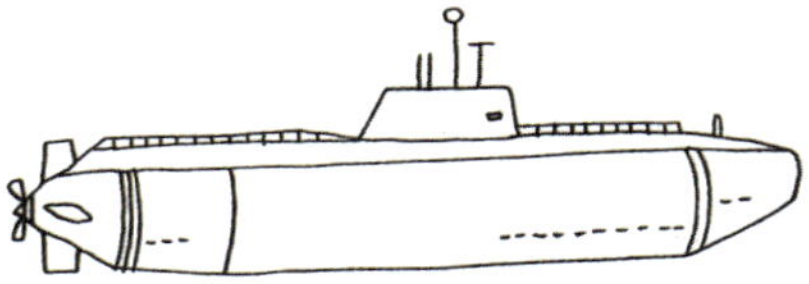

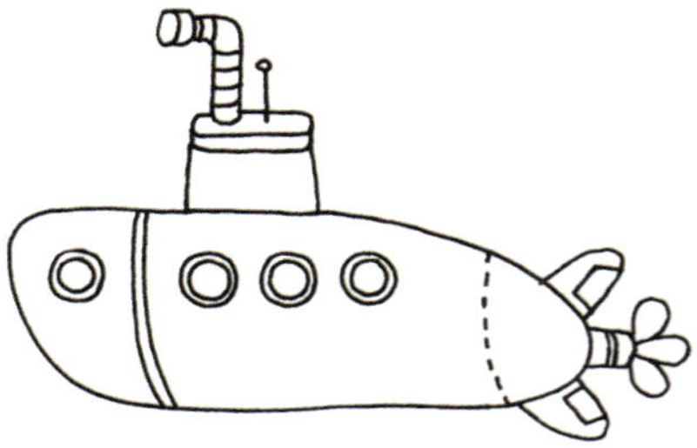

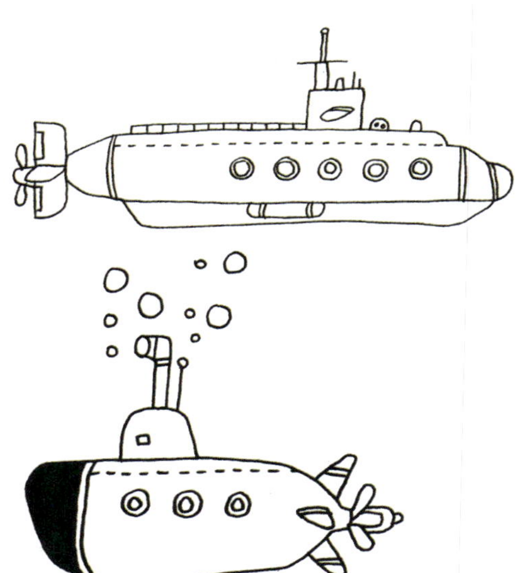
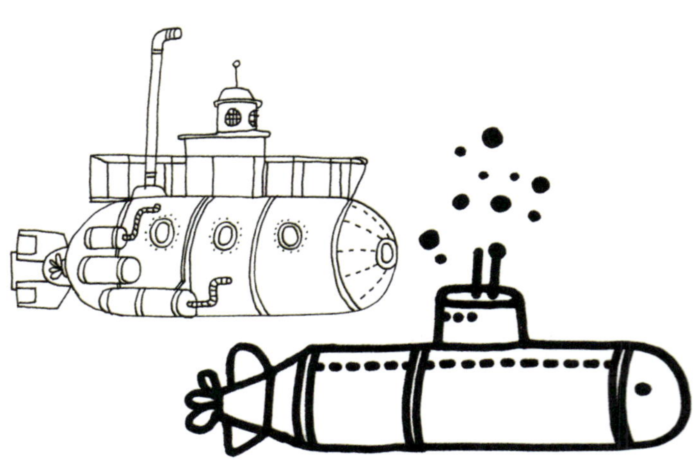

DRAW 20

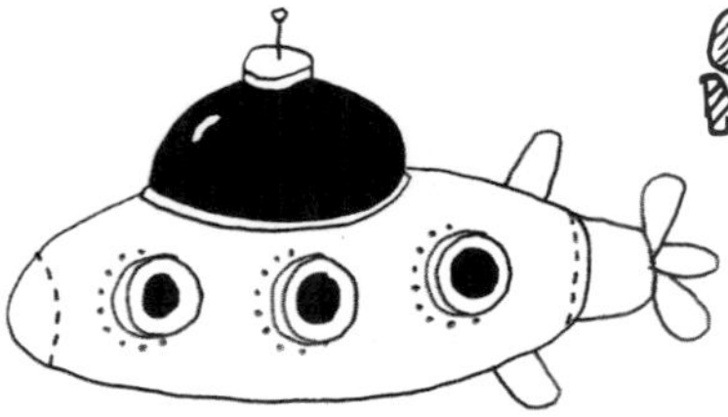

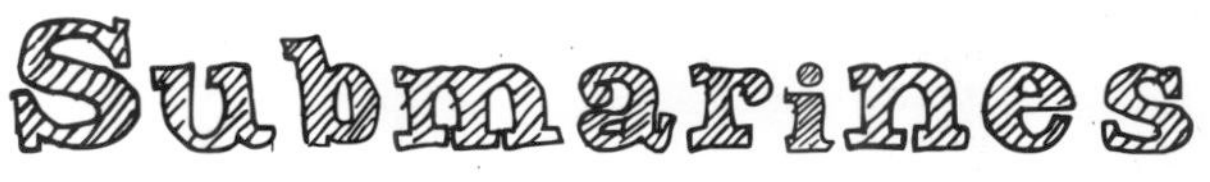

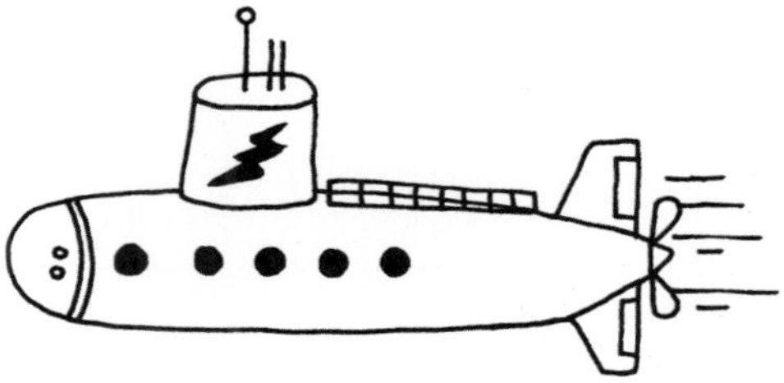

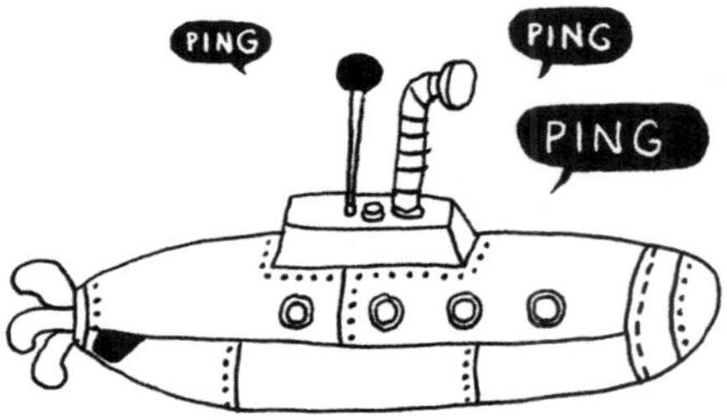

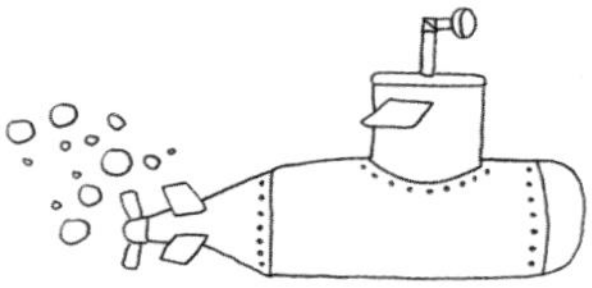

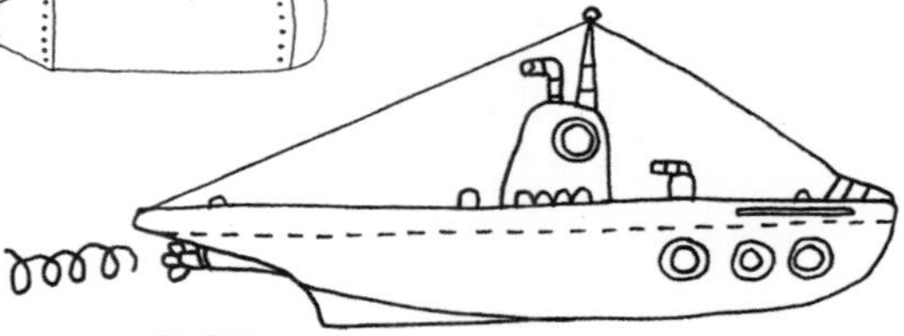

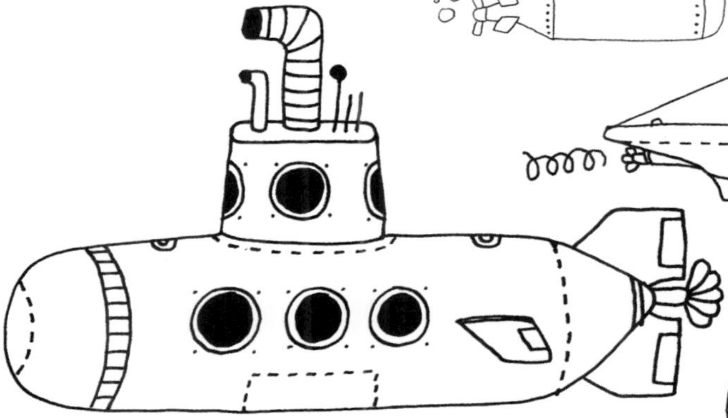

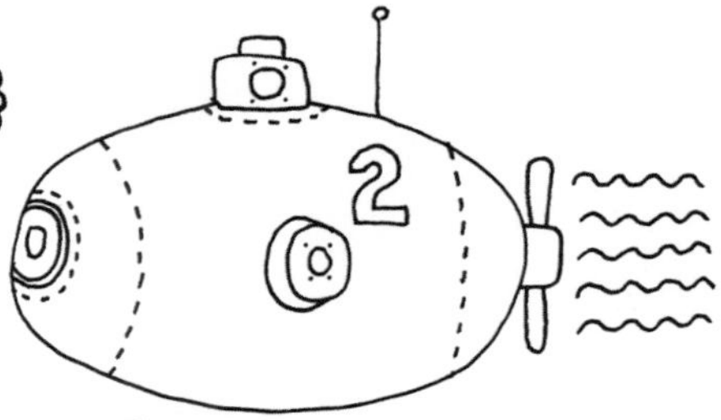

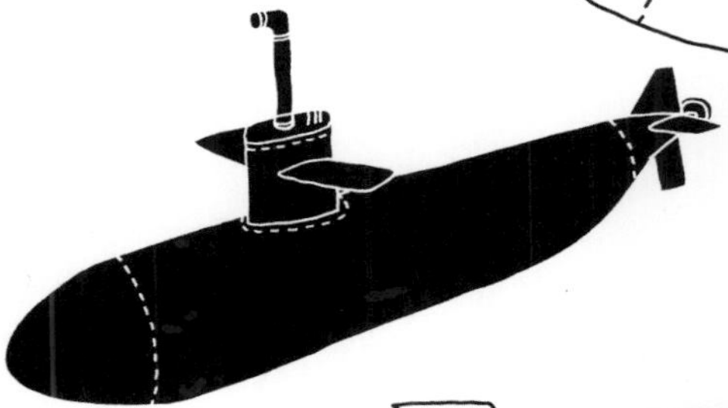

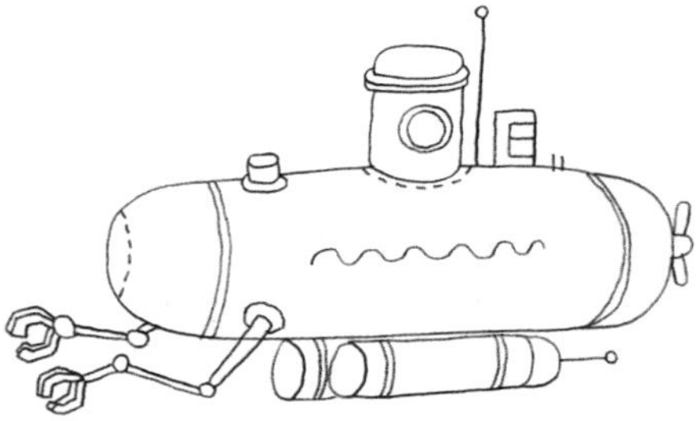

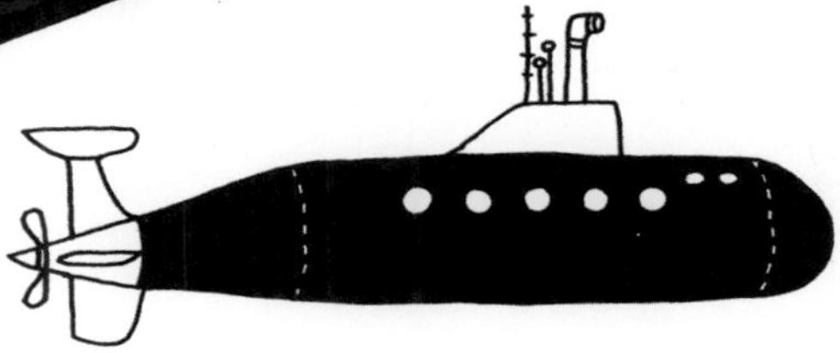

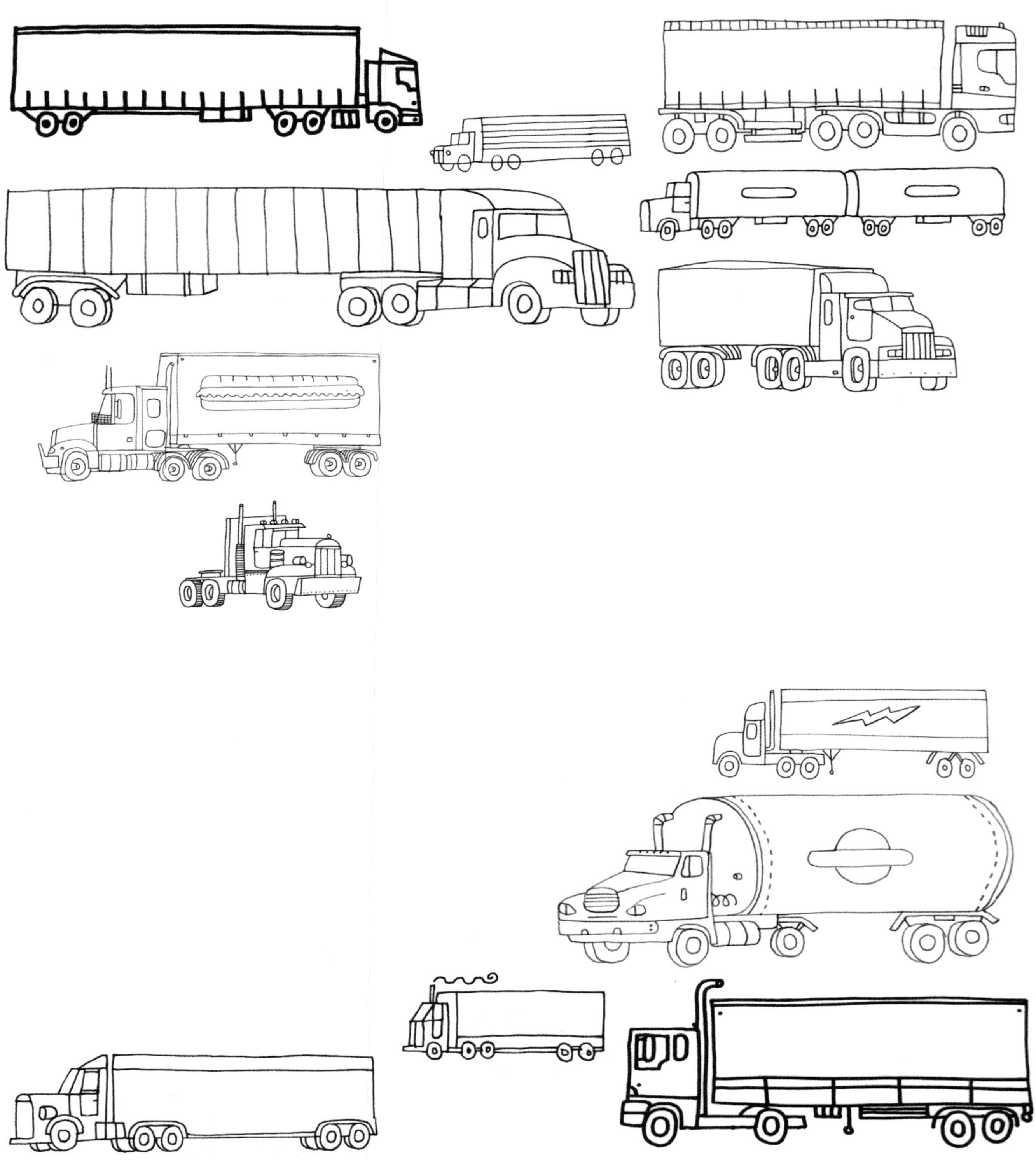

DRAW 20
SEMITRUCKS

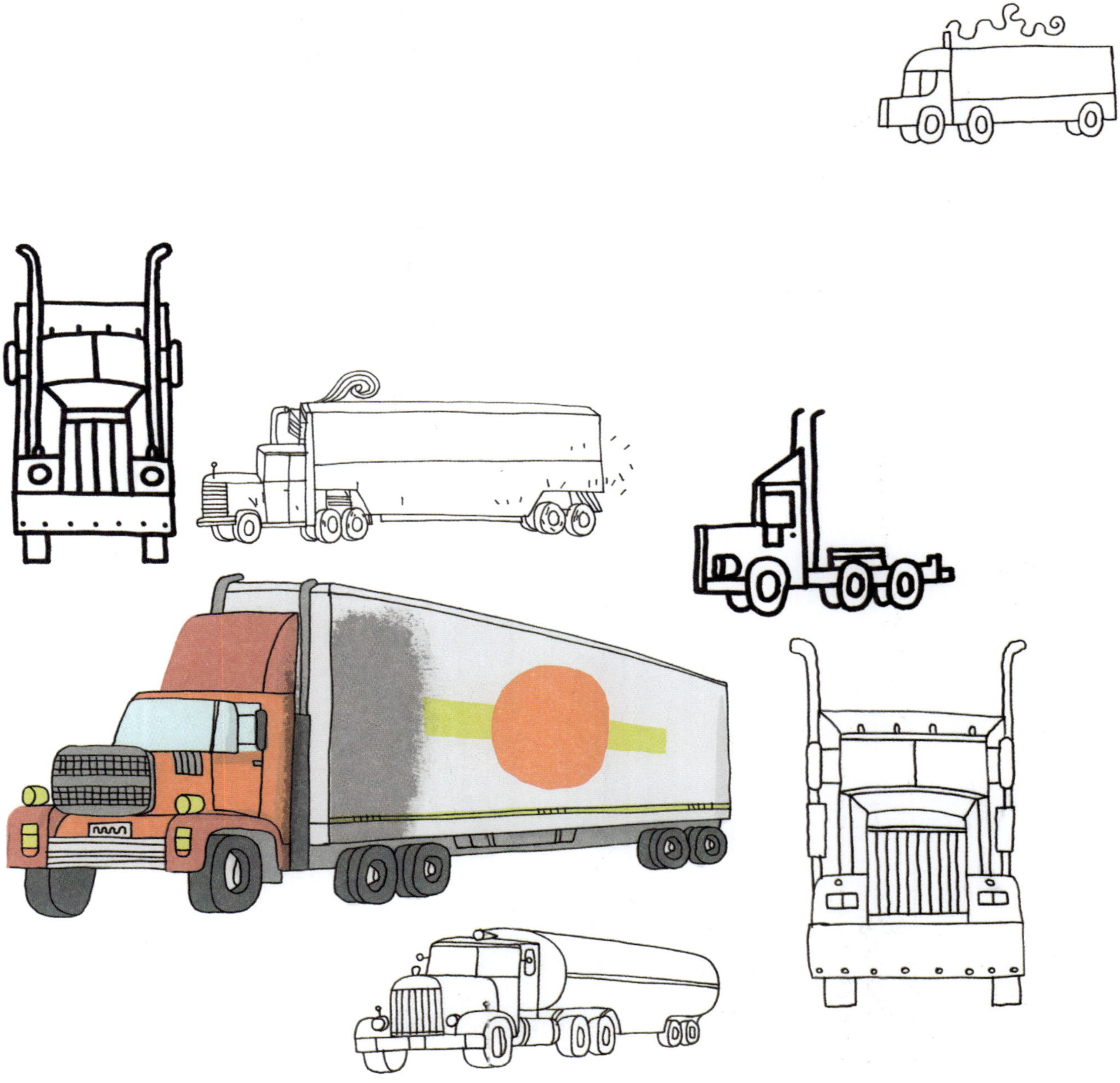

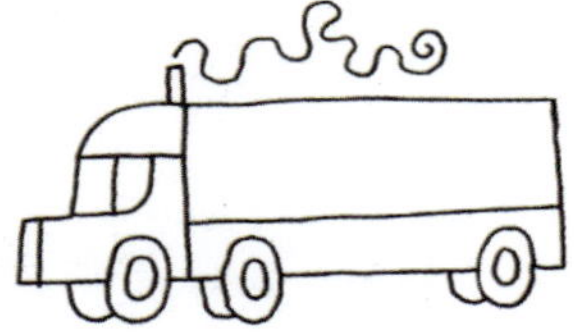

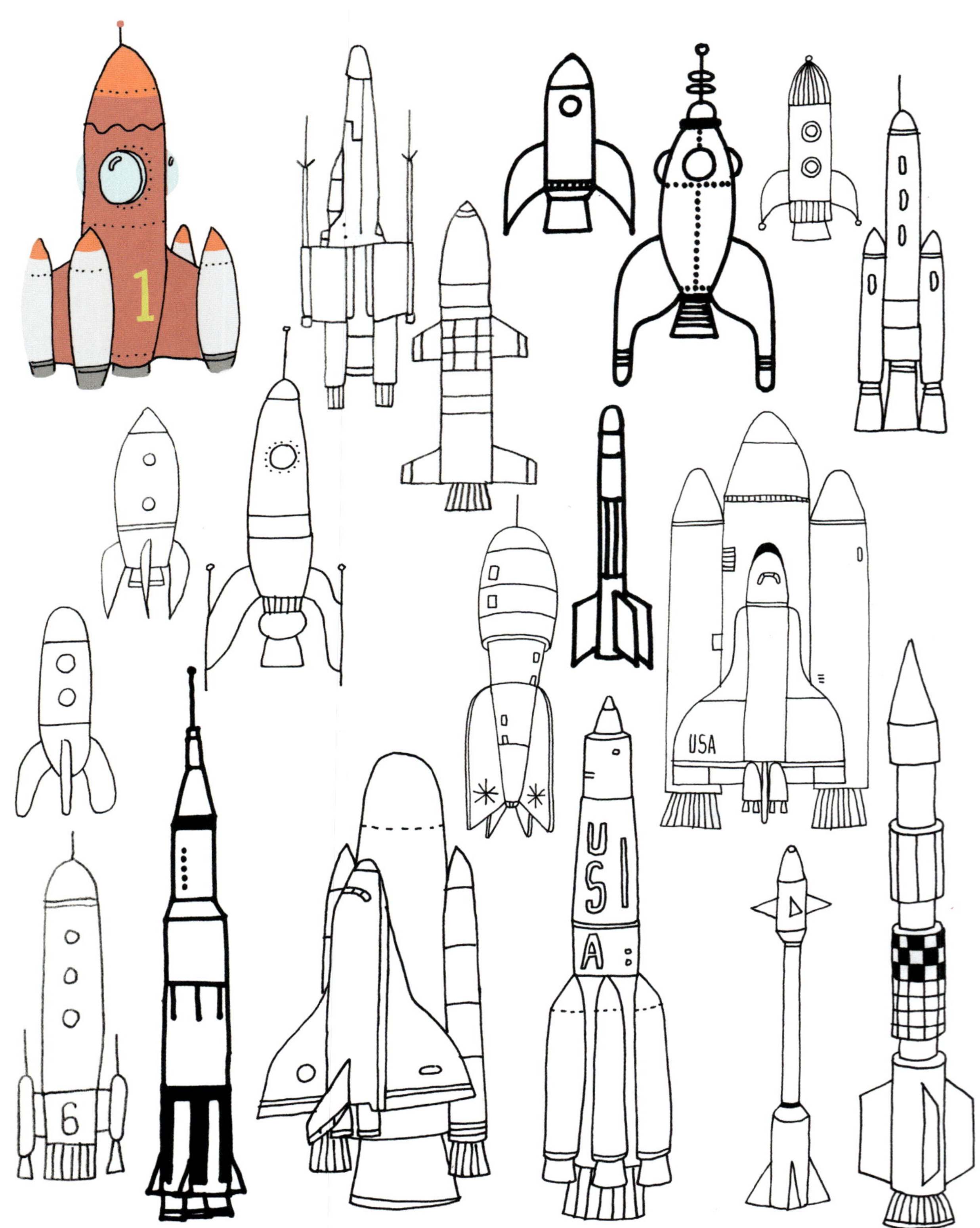

ROCKET SHIPS

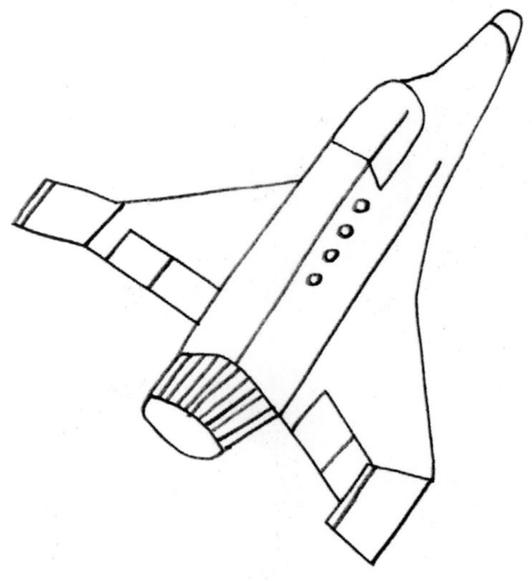

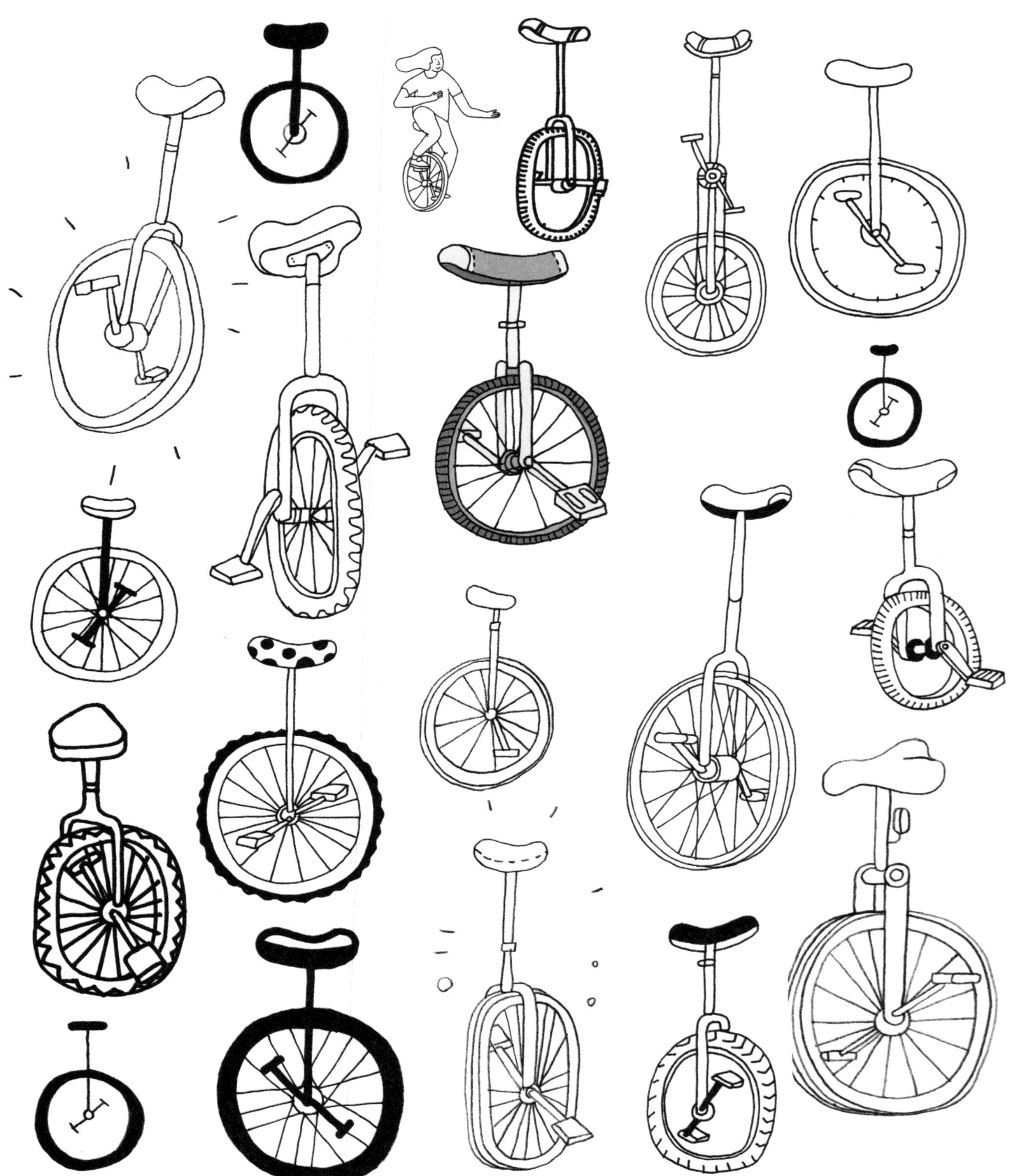

Unicycles

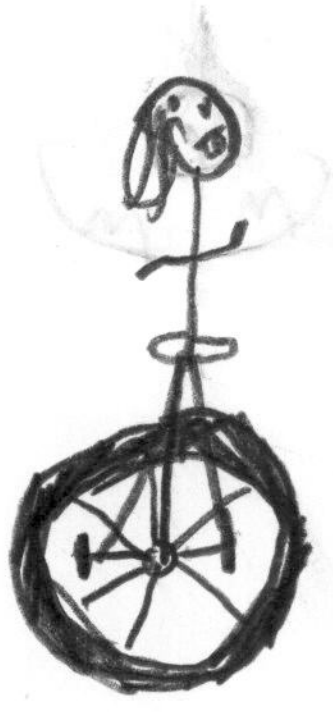

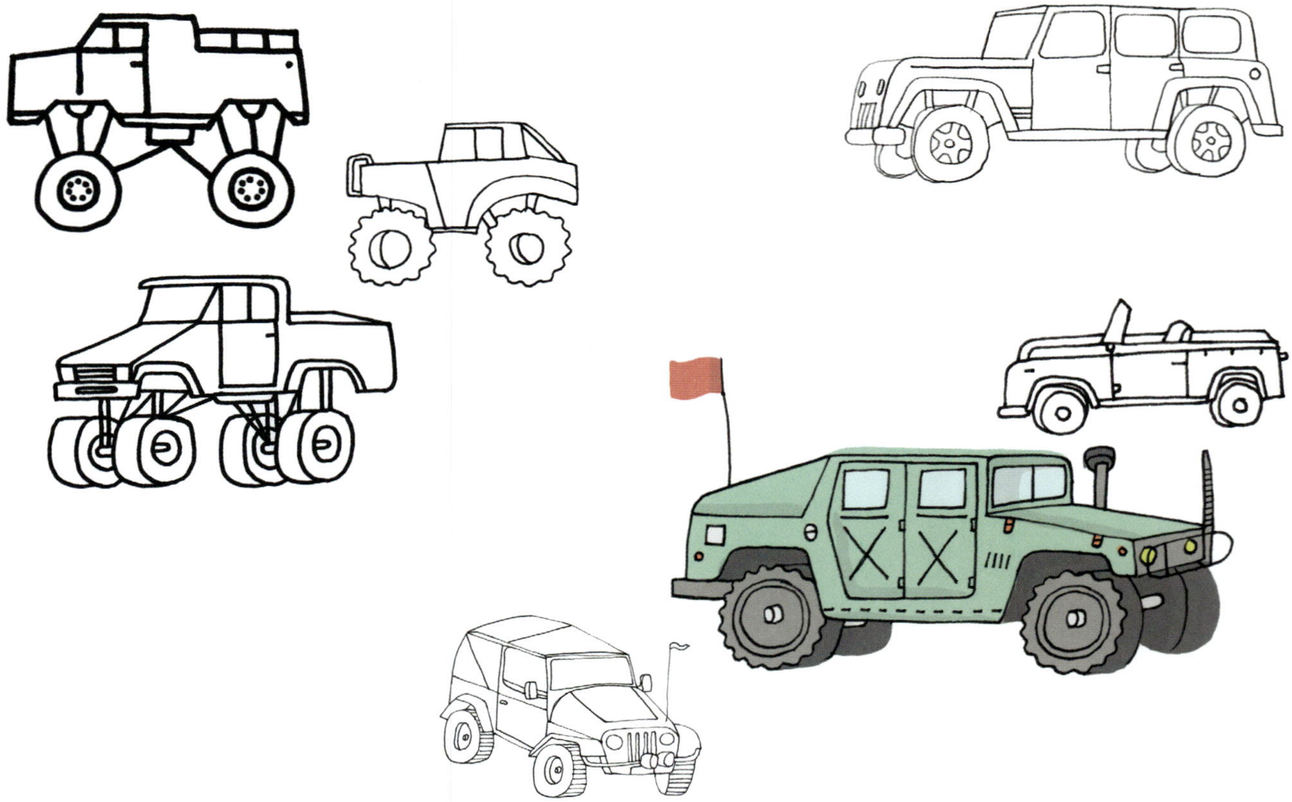

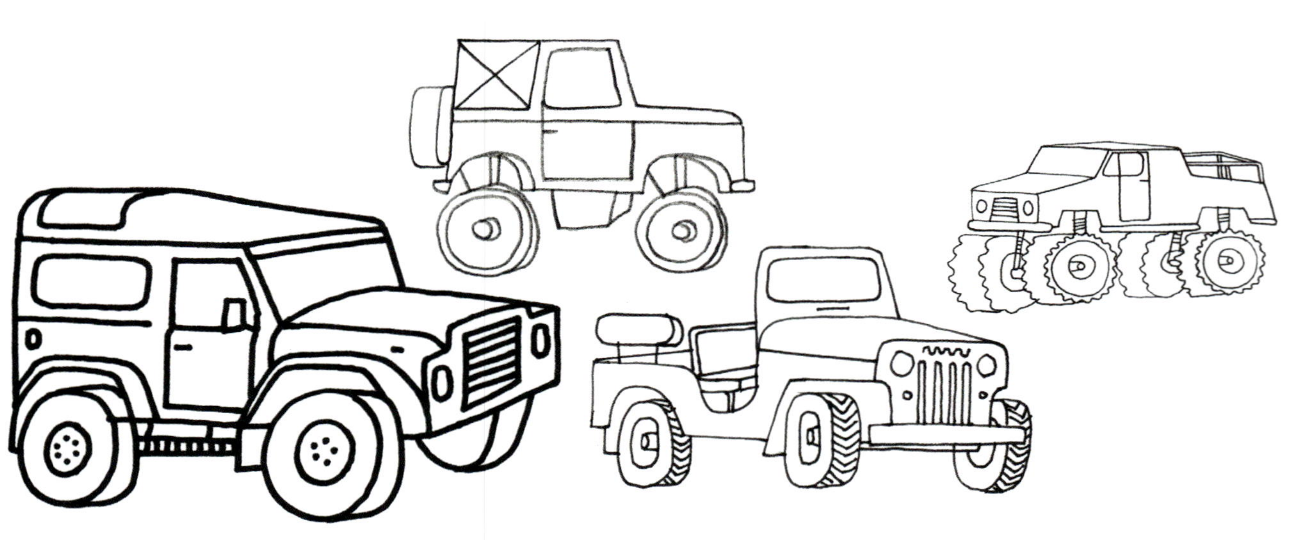

DRAW 20
FOUR-WHEELERS

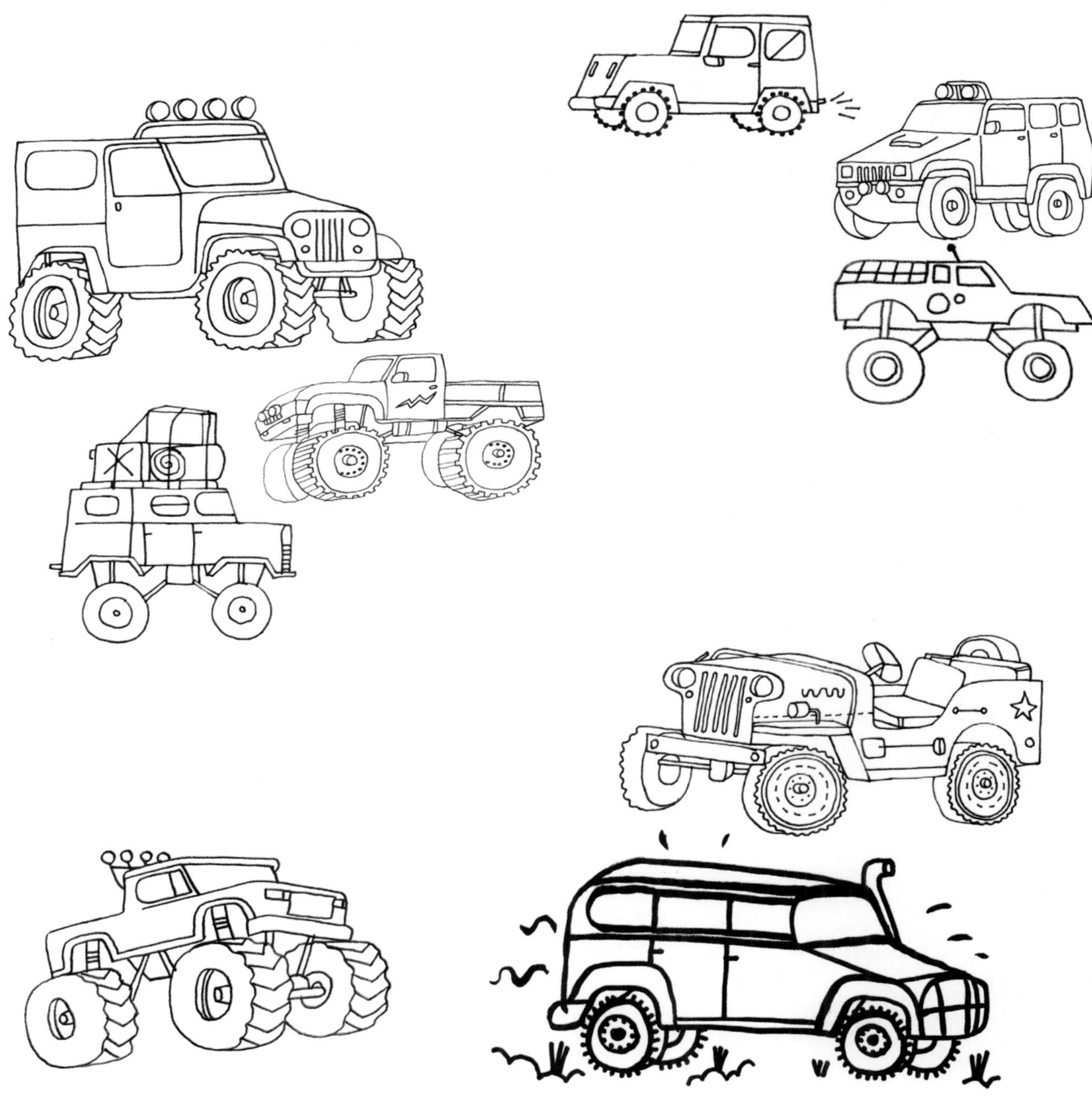

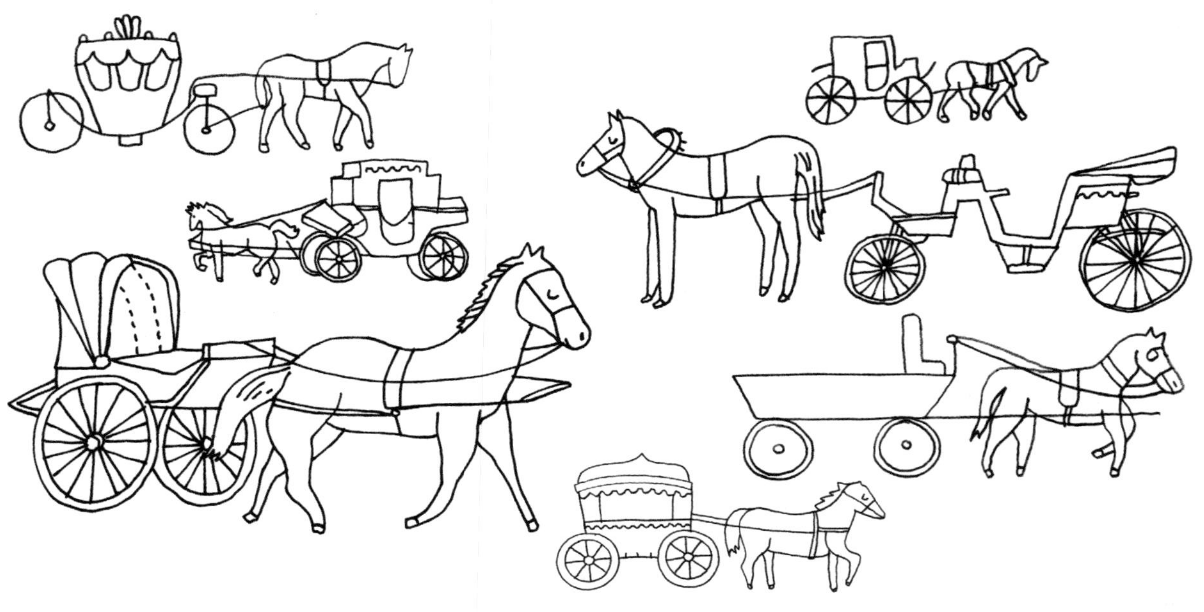

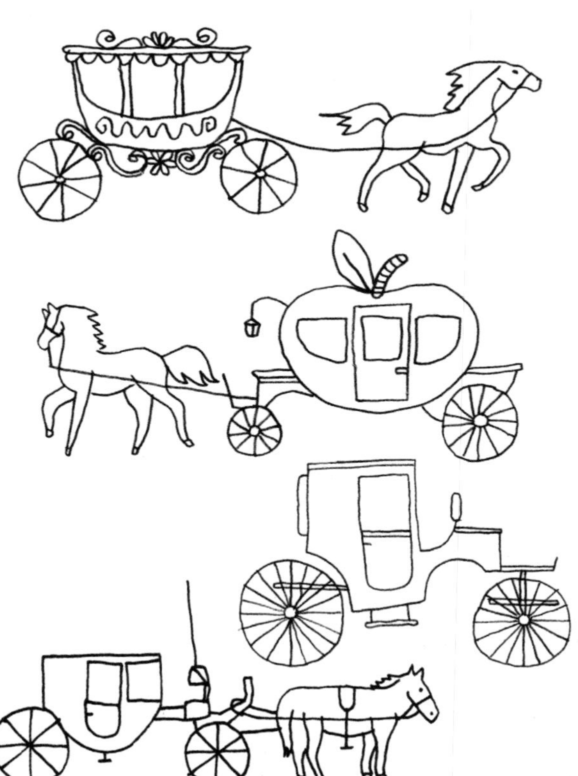

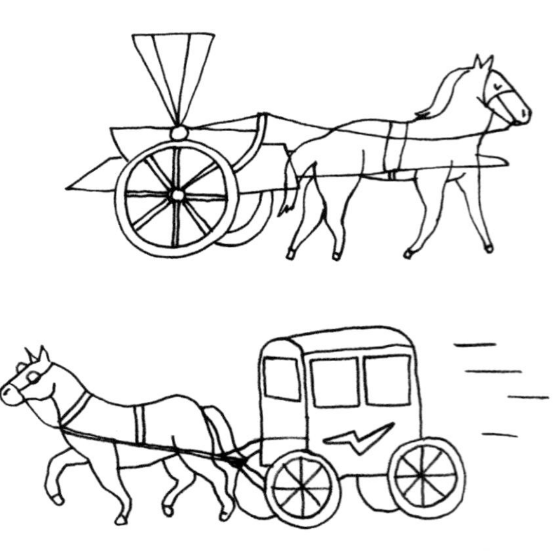

Carriages

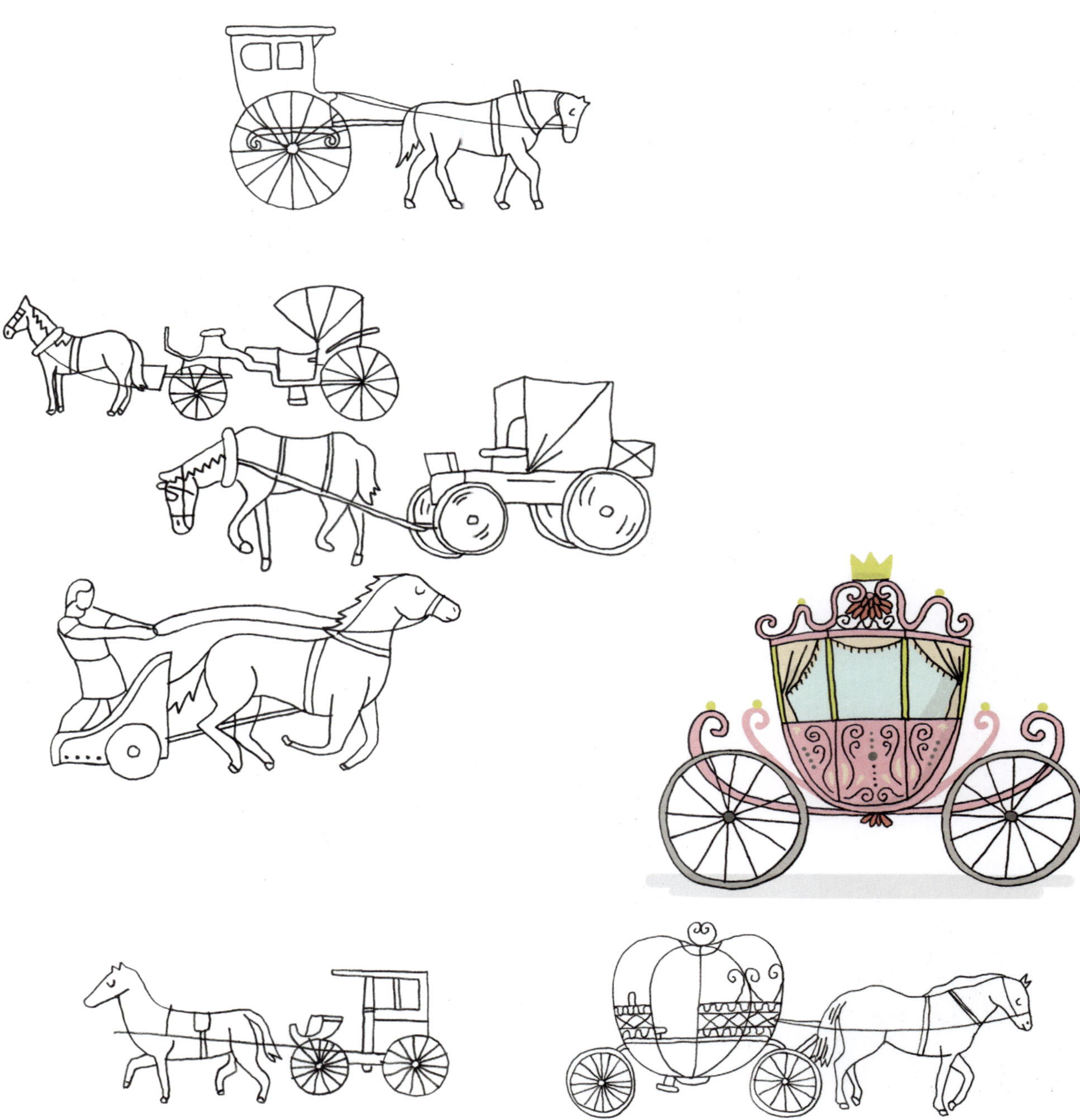

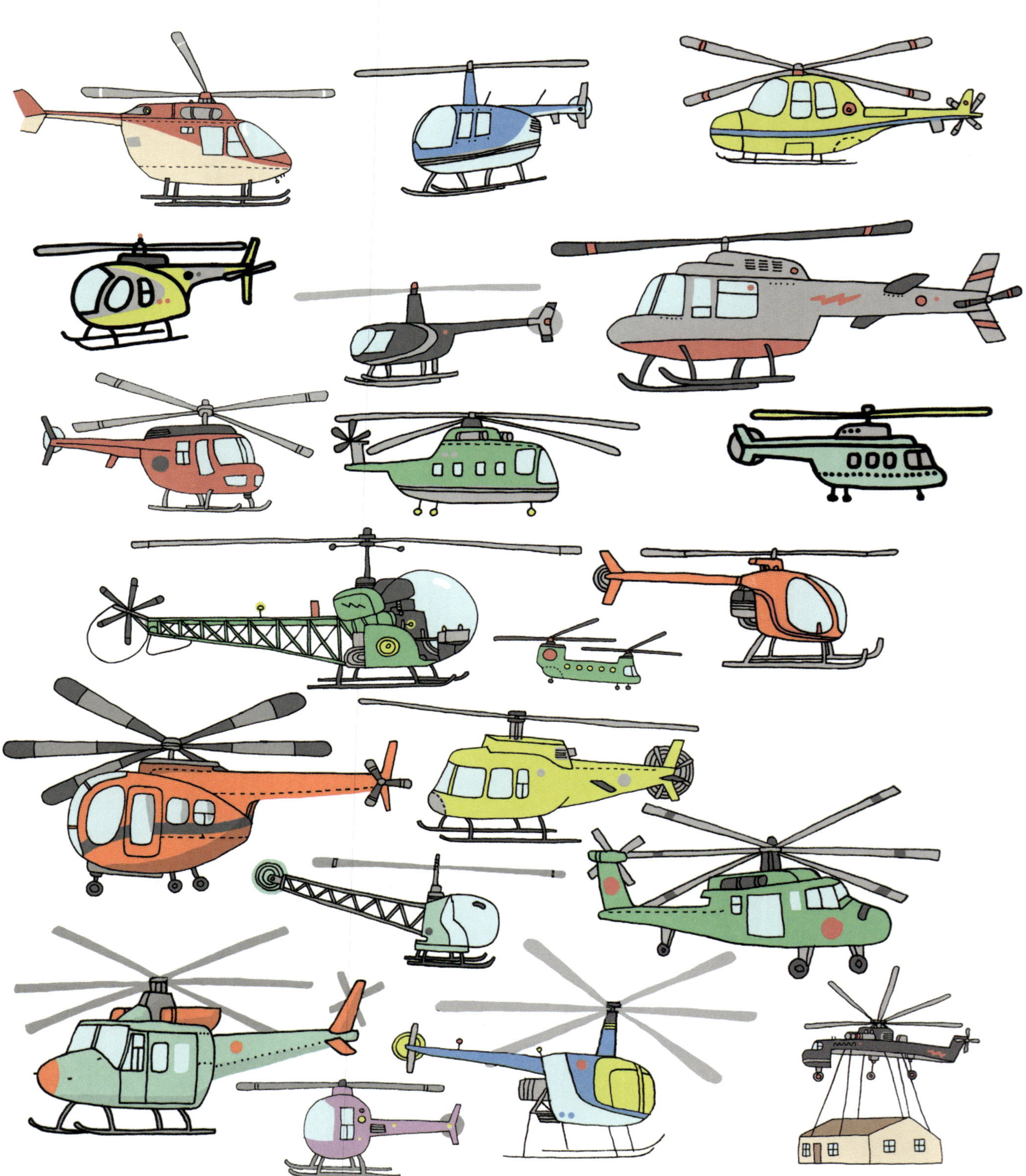

DRAW 20

Helicopters

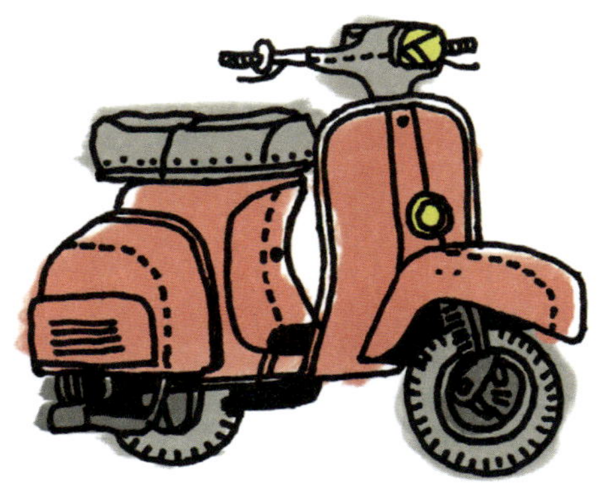

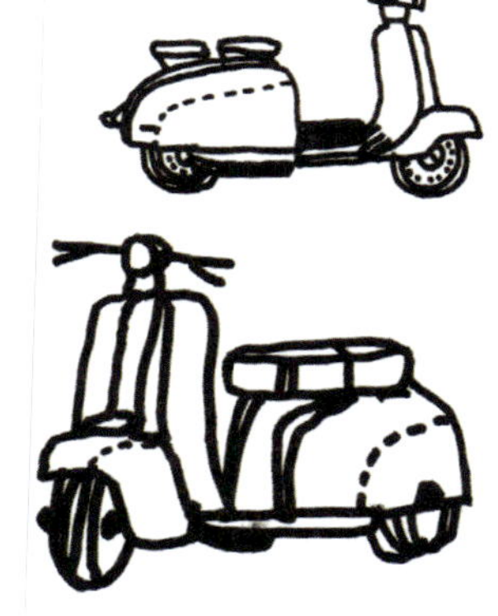

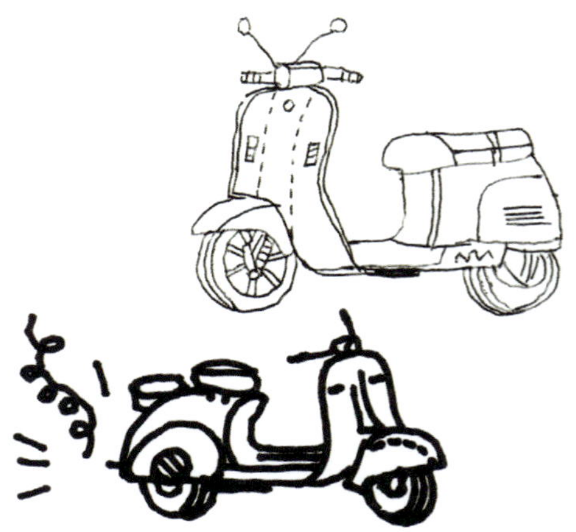

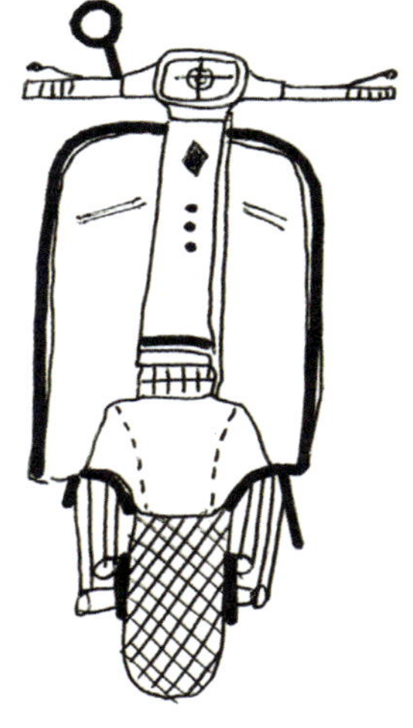

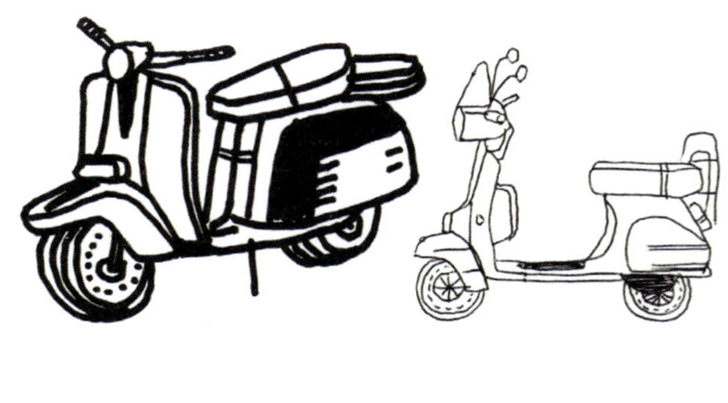

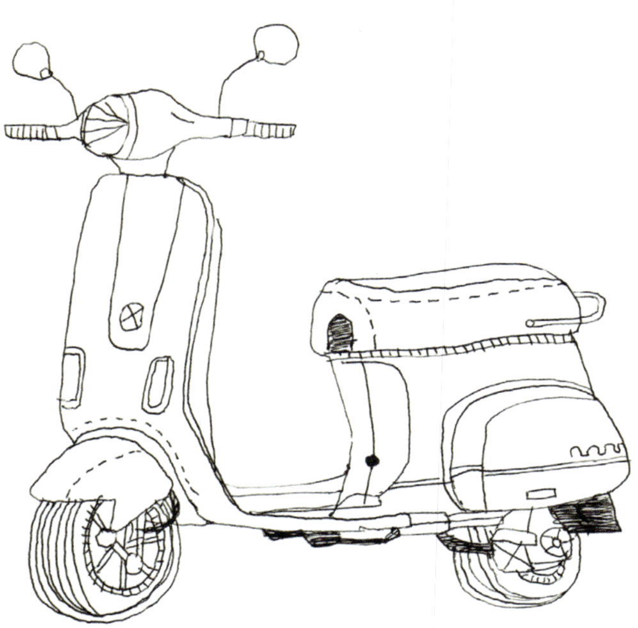

DRAW 20
Motor Scooters

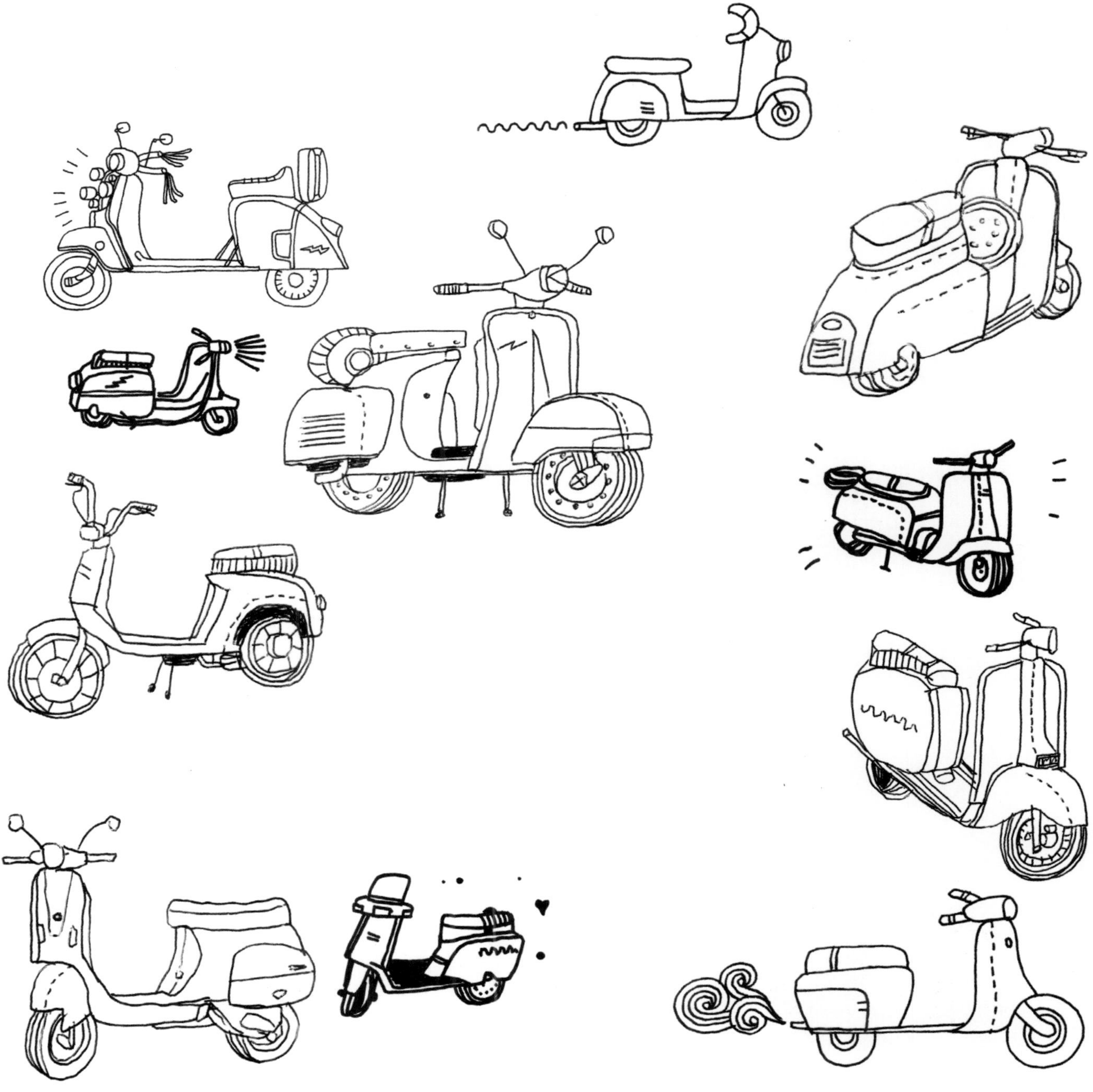

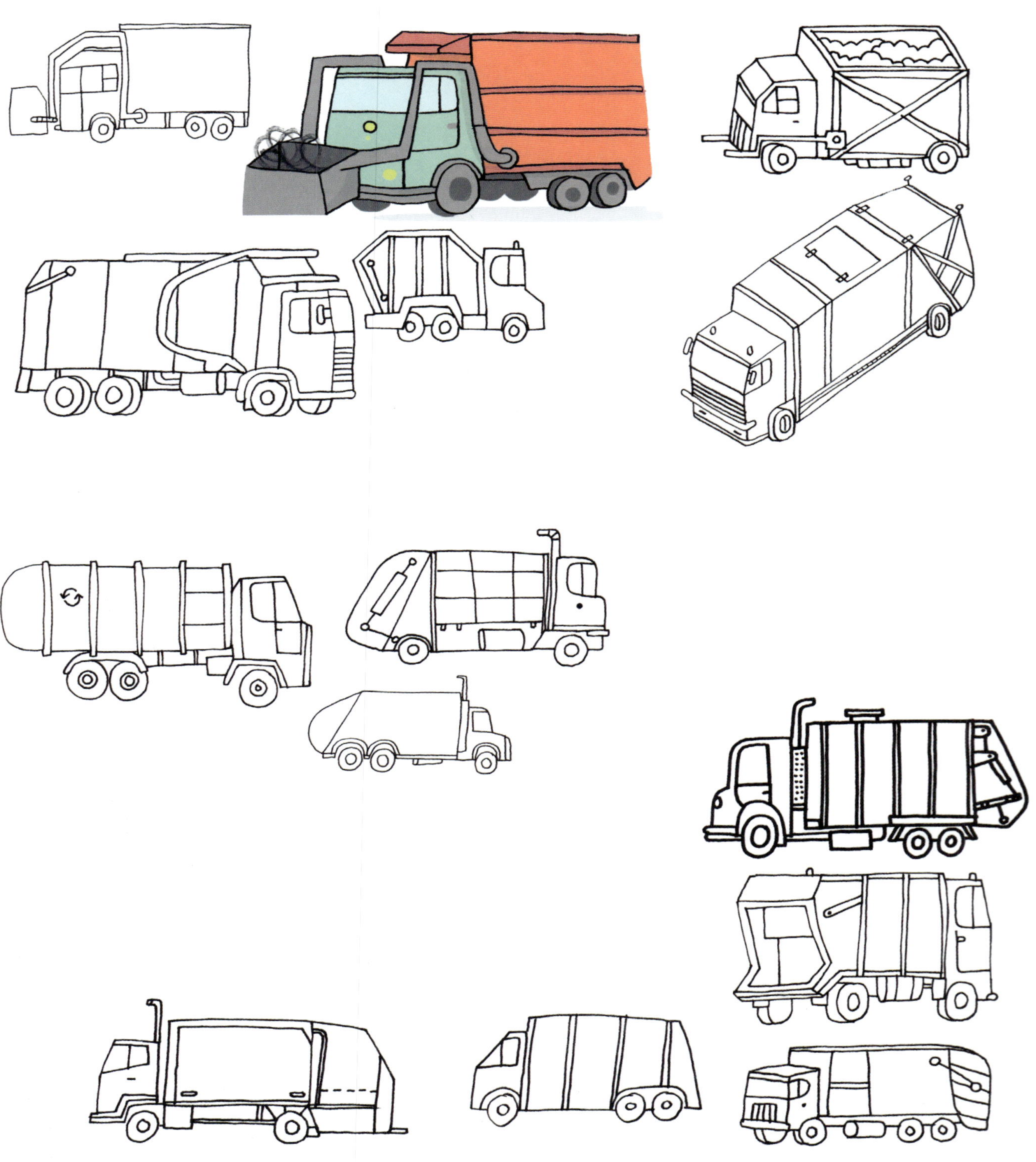

DRAW 20
GARBAGE TRUCKS

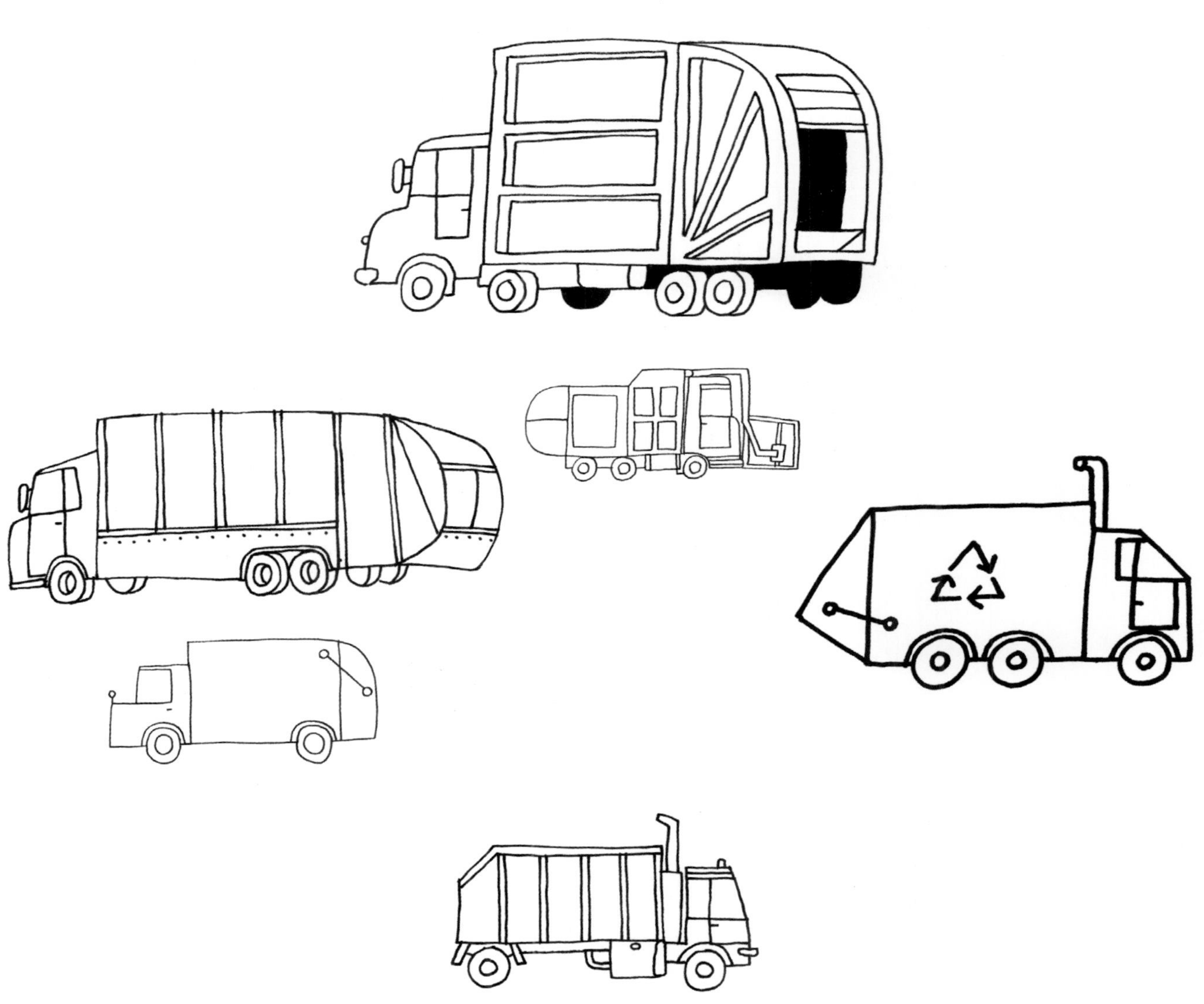

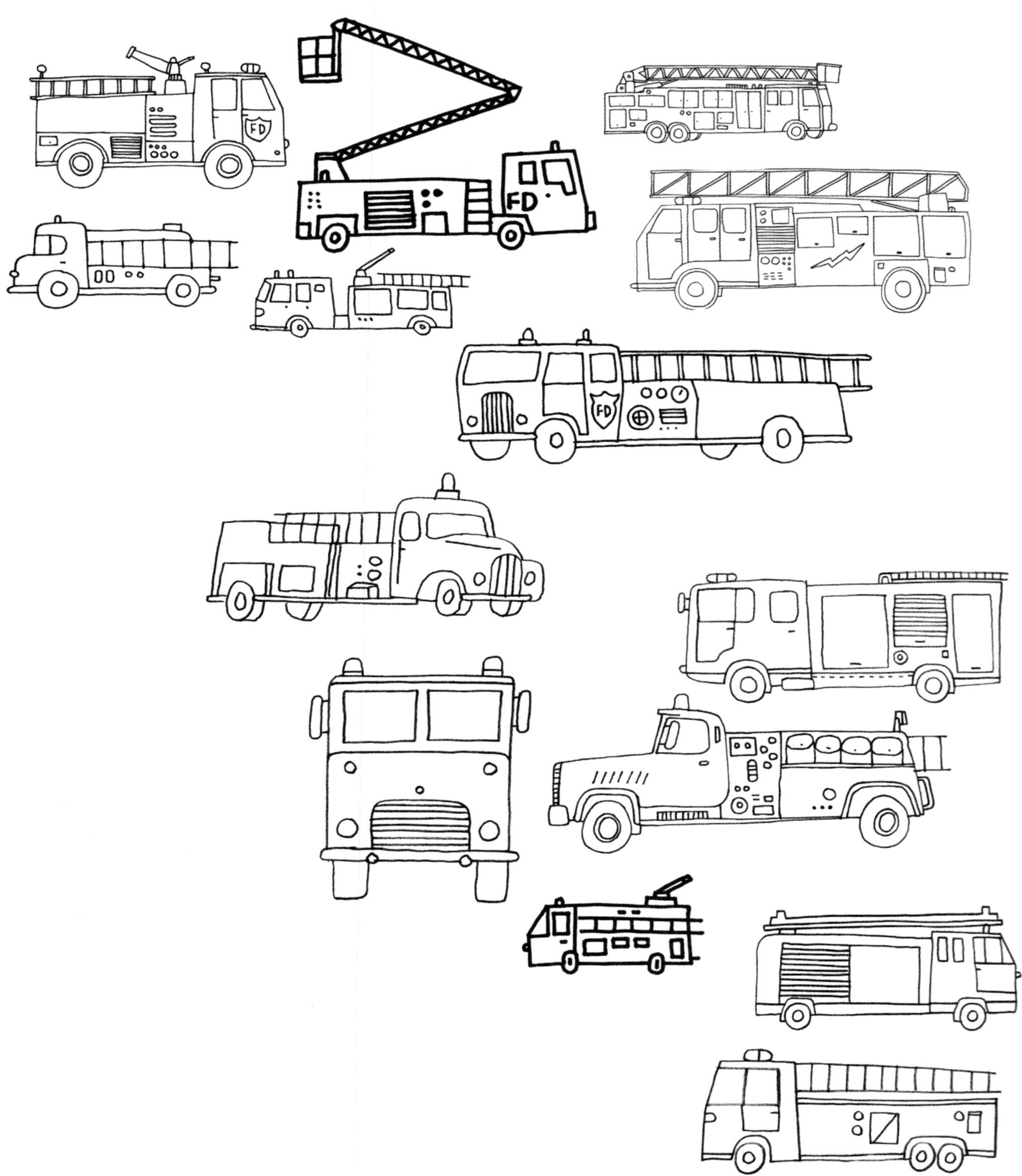

FIRE ENGINES

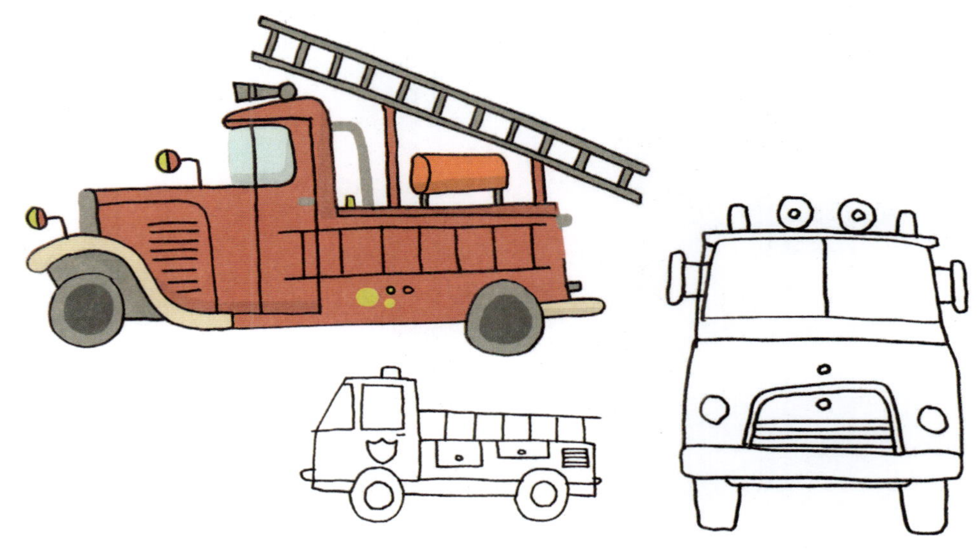

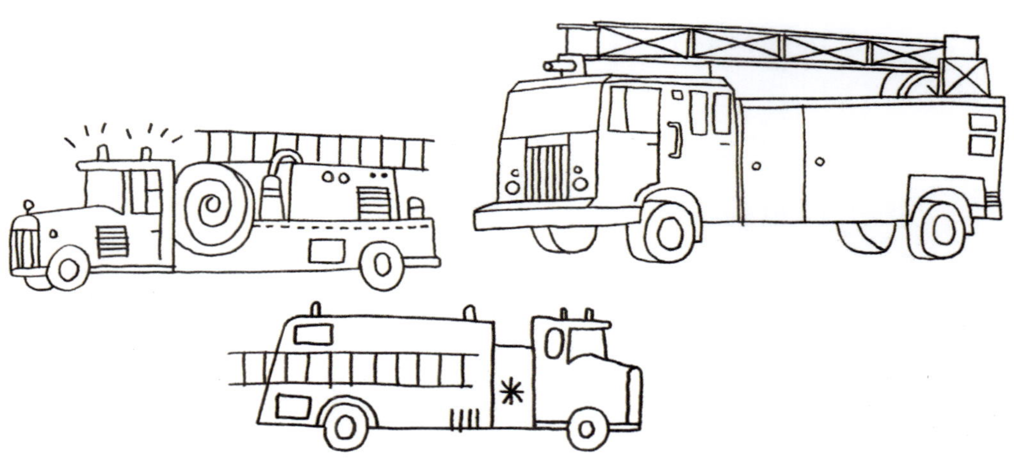

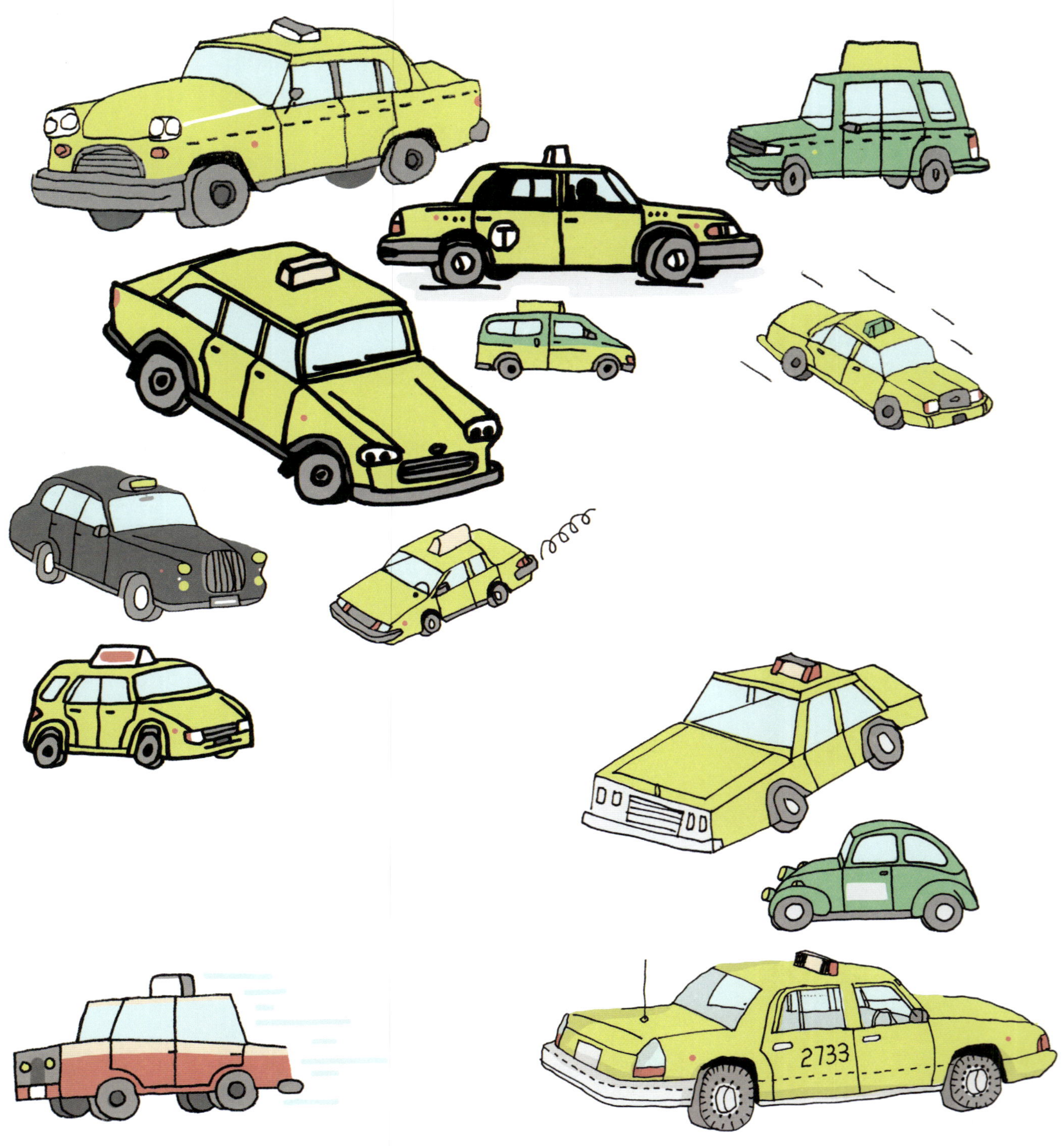
2733

DRAW 20

taxis

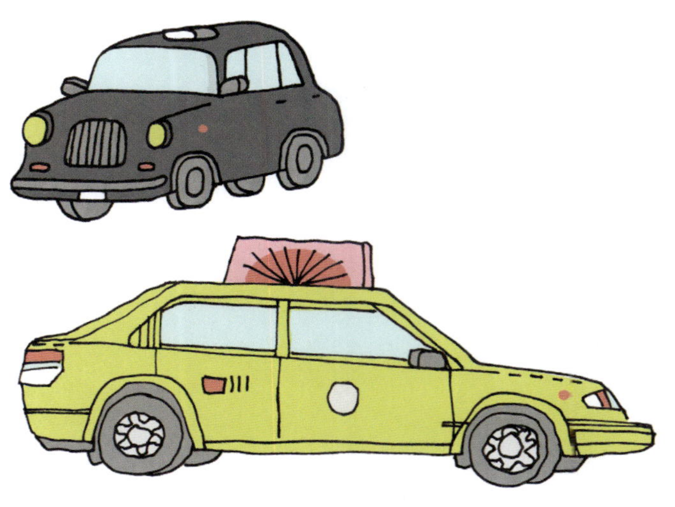

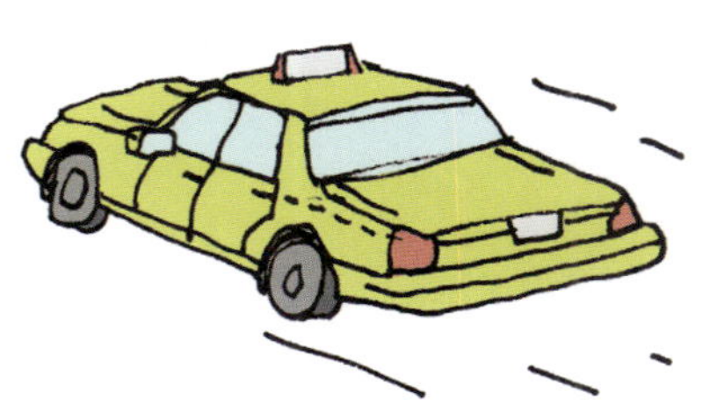

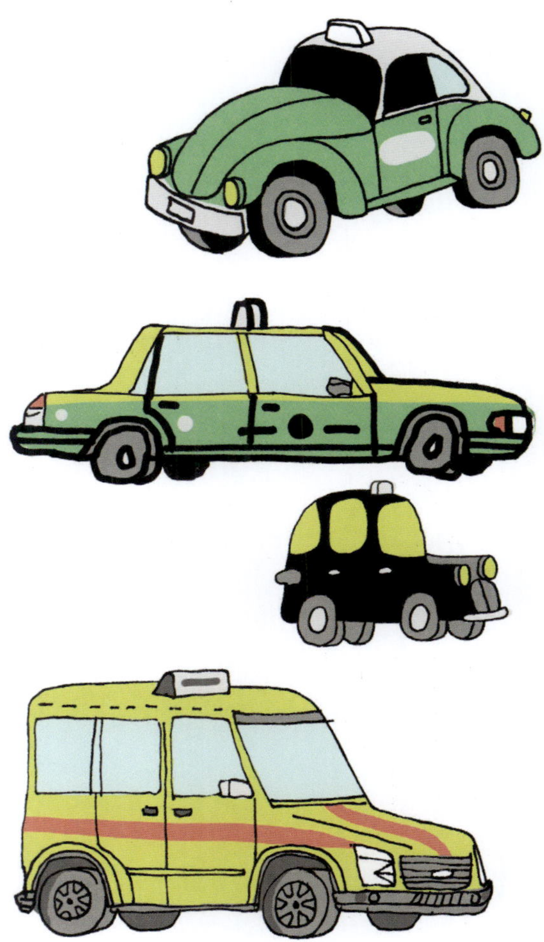

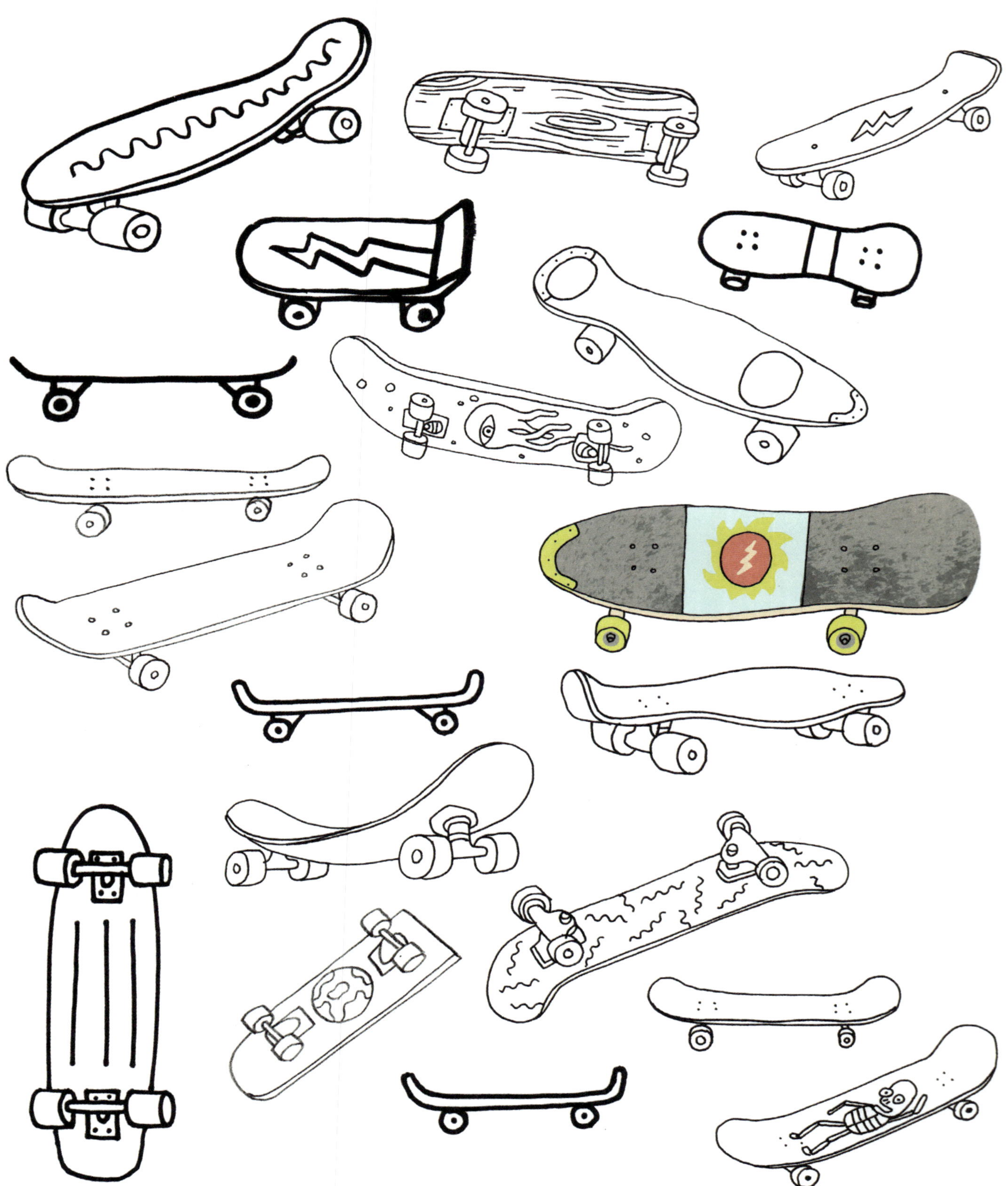

DRAW 20
SKATEBOARDS

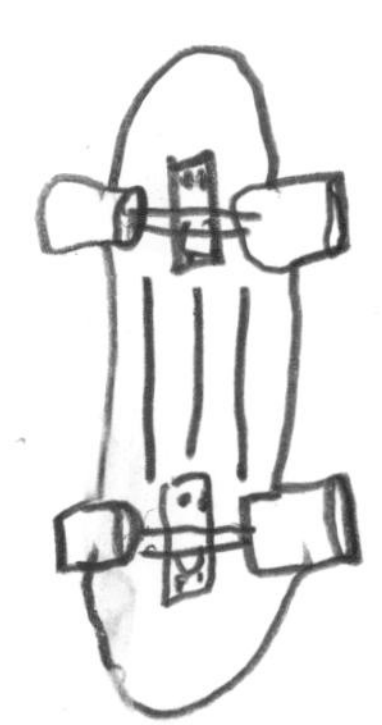

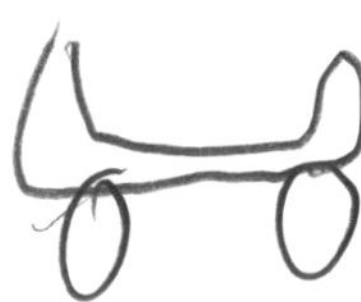

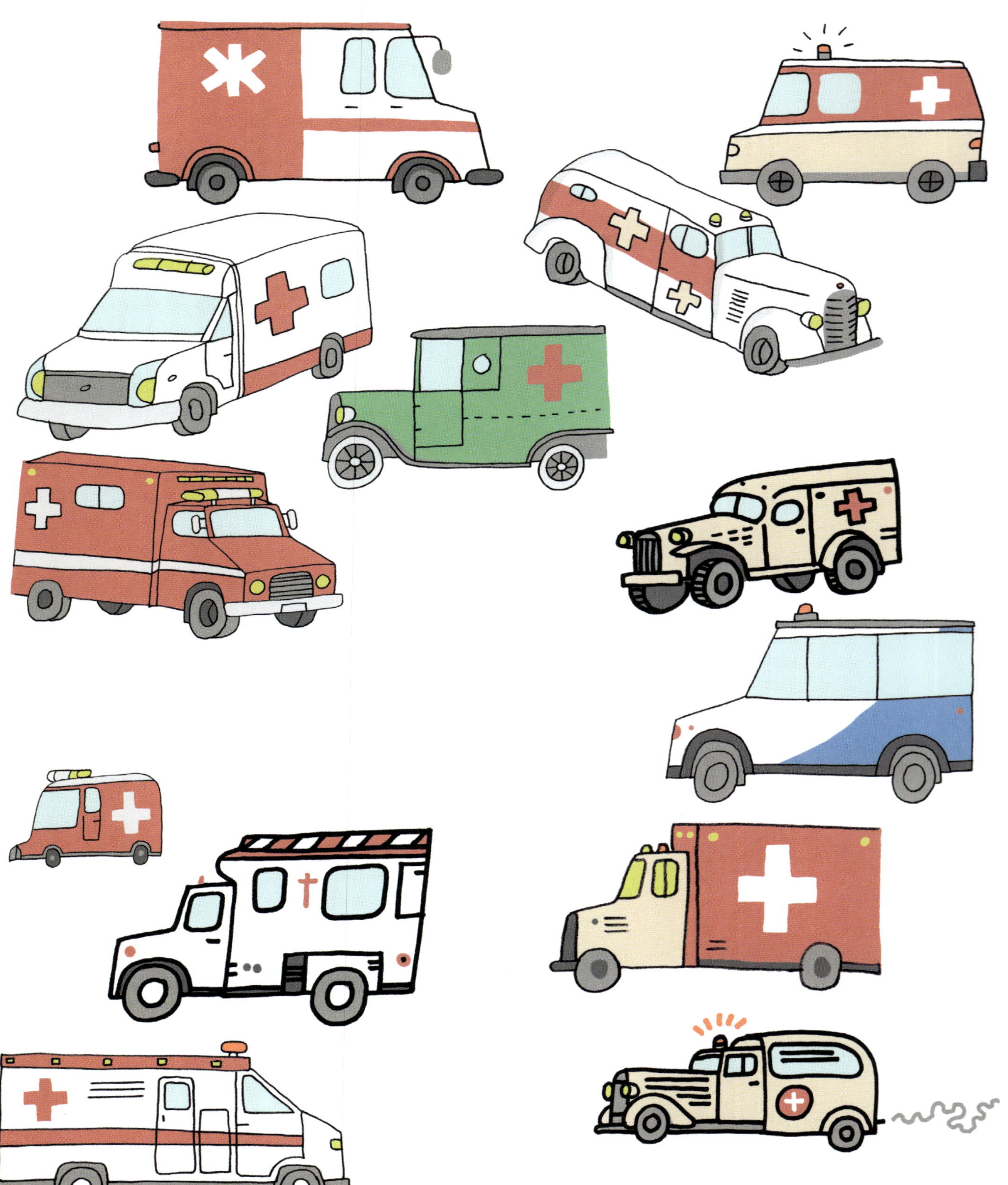

AMBULANCES

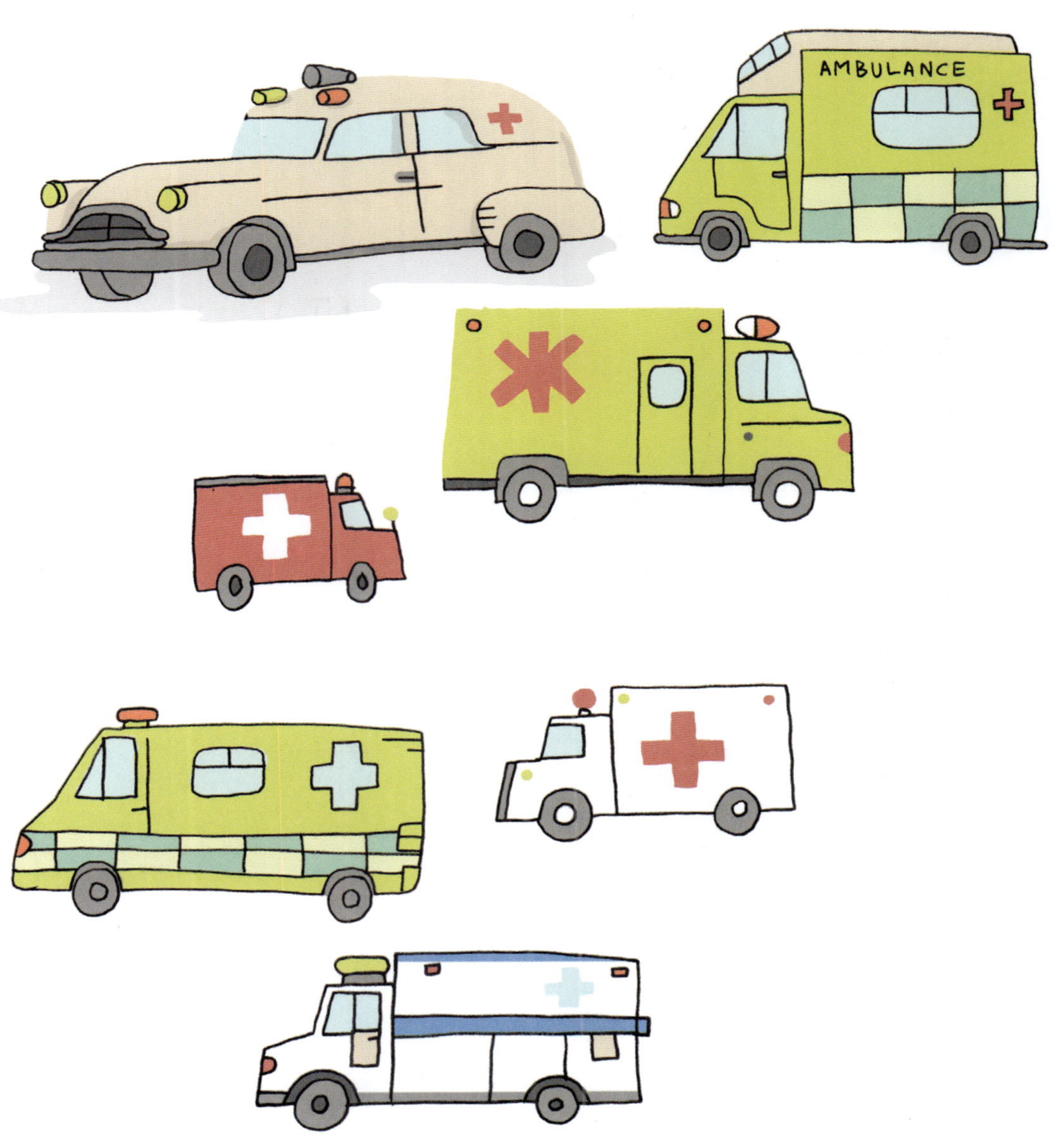

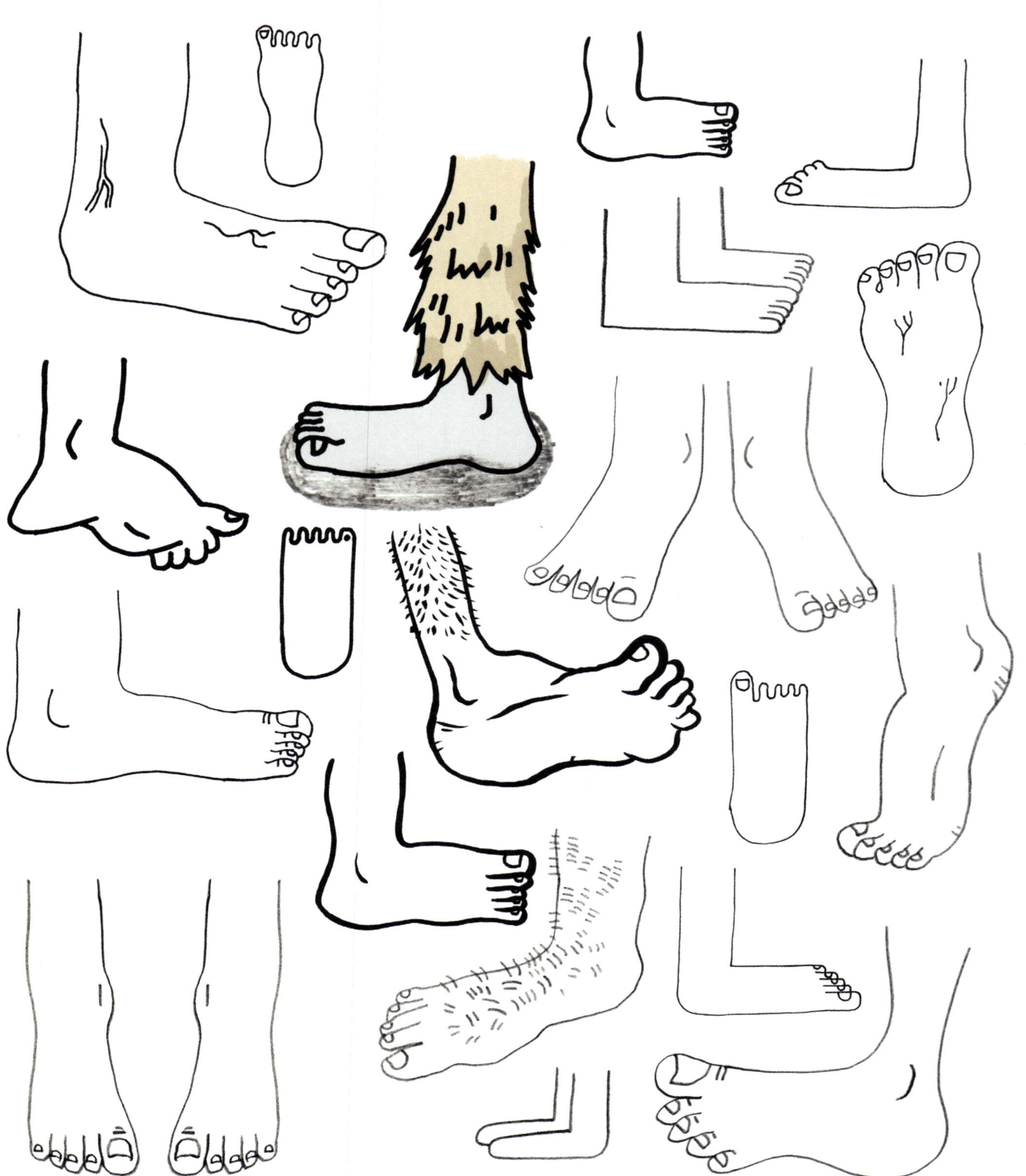

DRAW 20
Feet

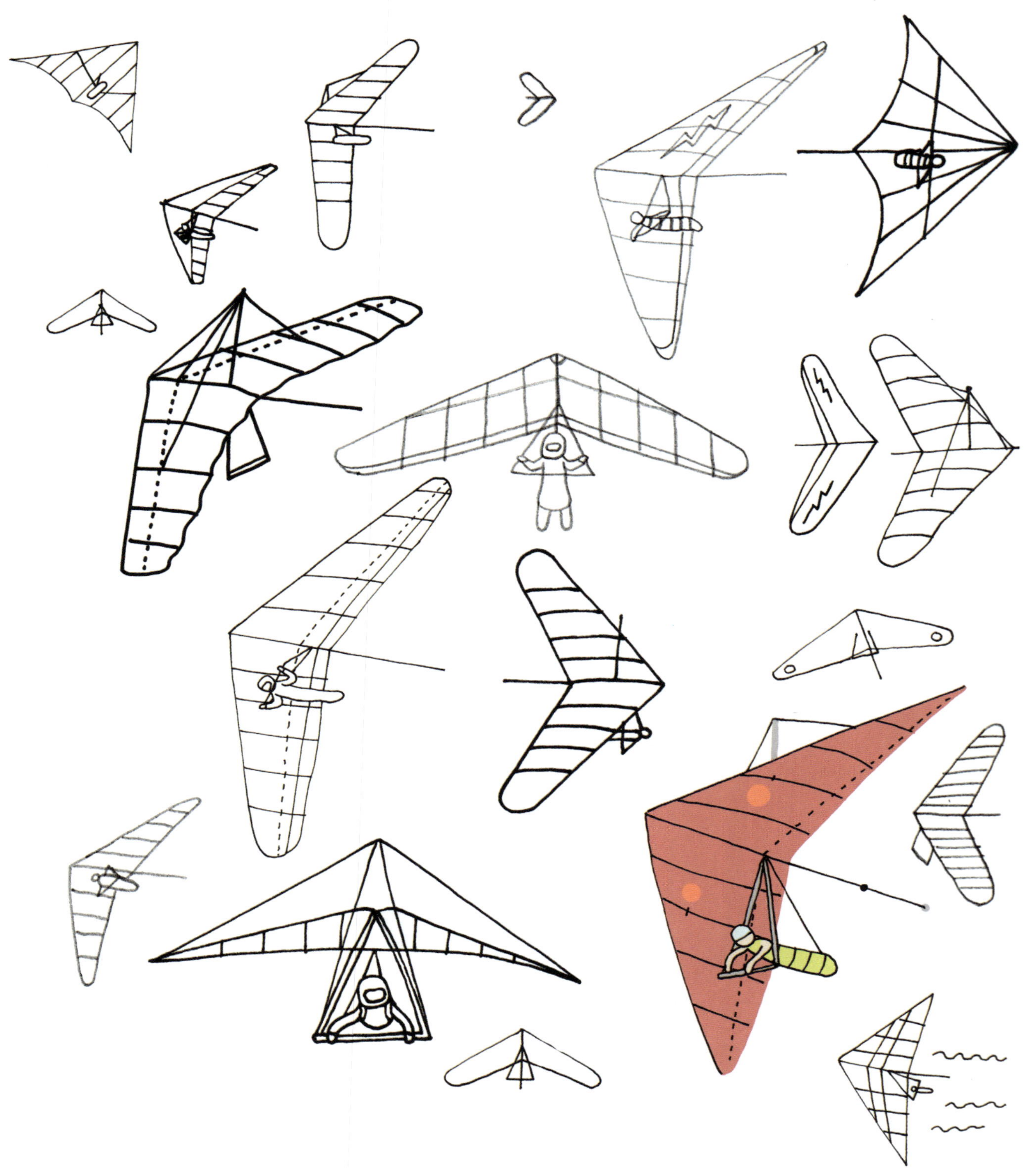

DRAW 20
Hang Gliders

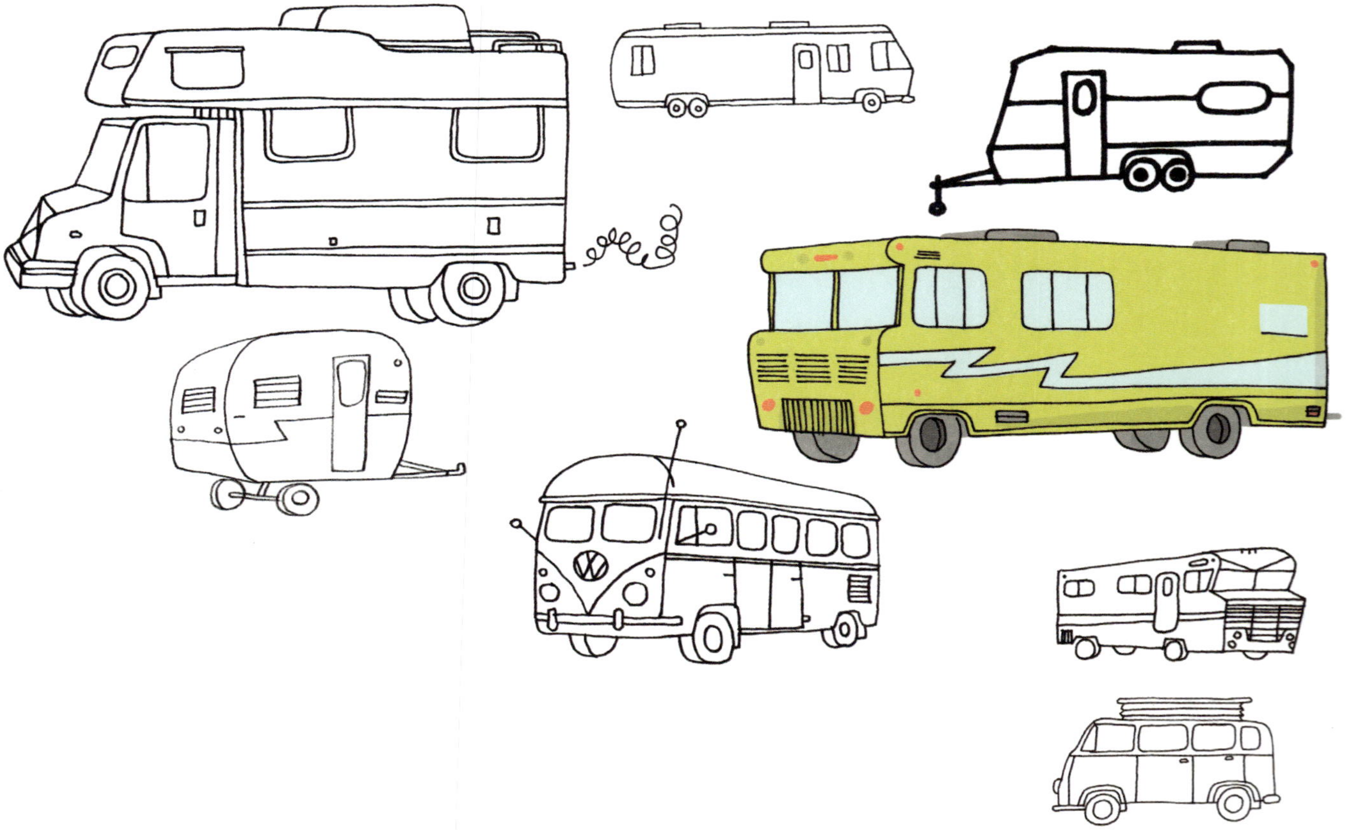

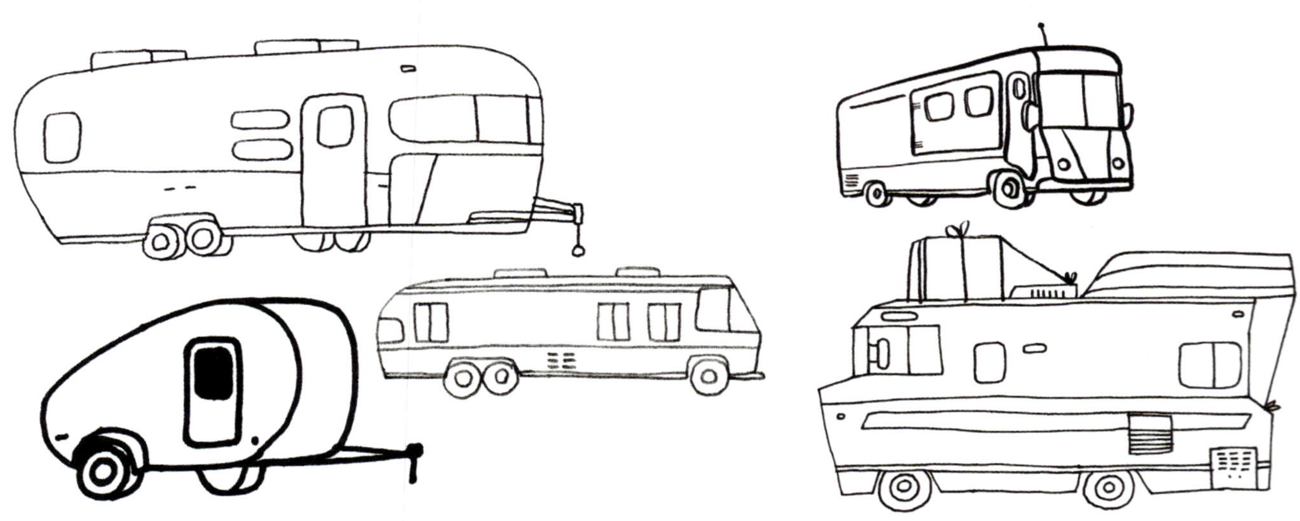

DRAW 20
RECREATIONAL VEHICLES

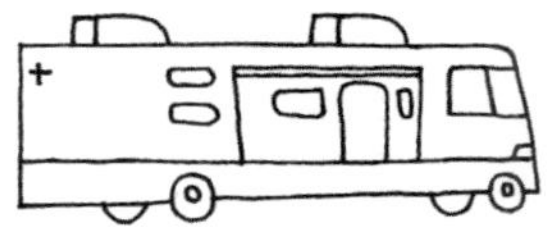

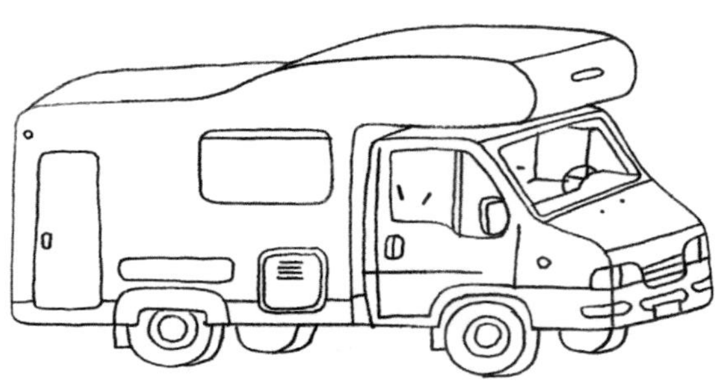

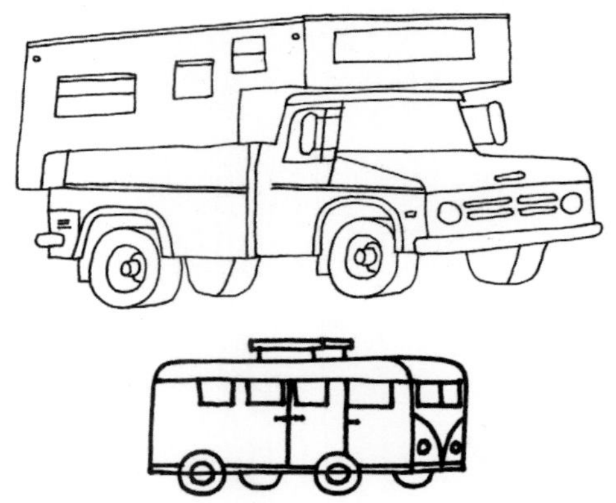

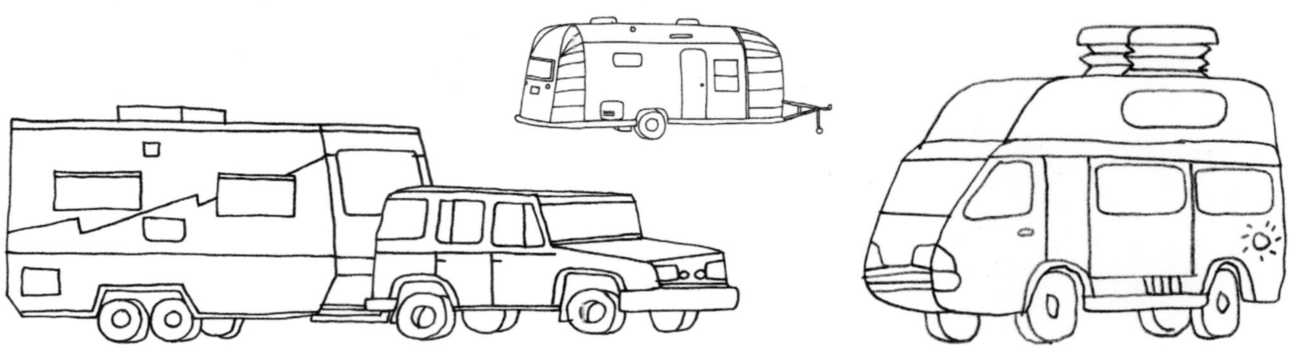

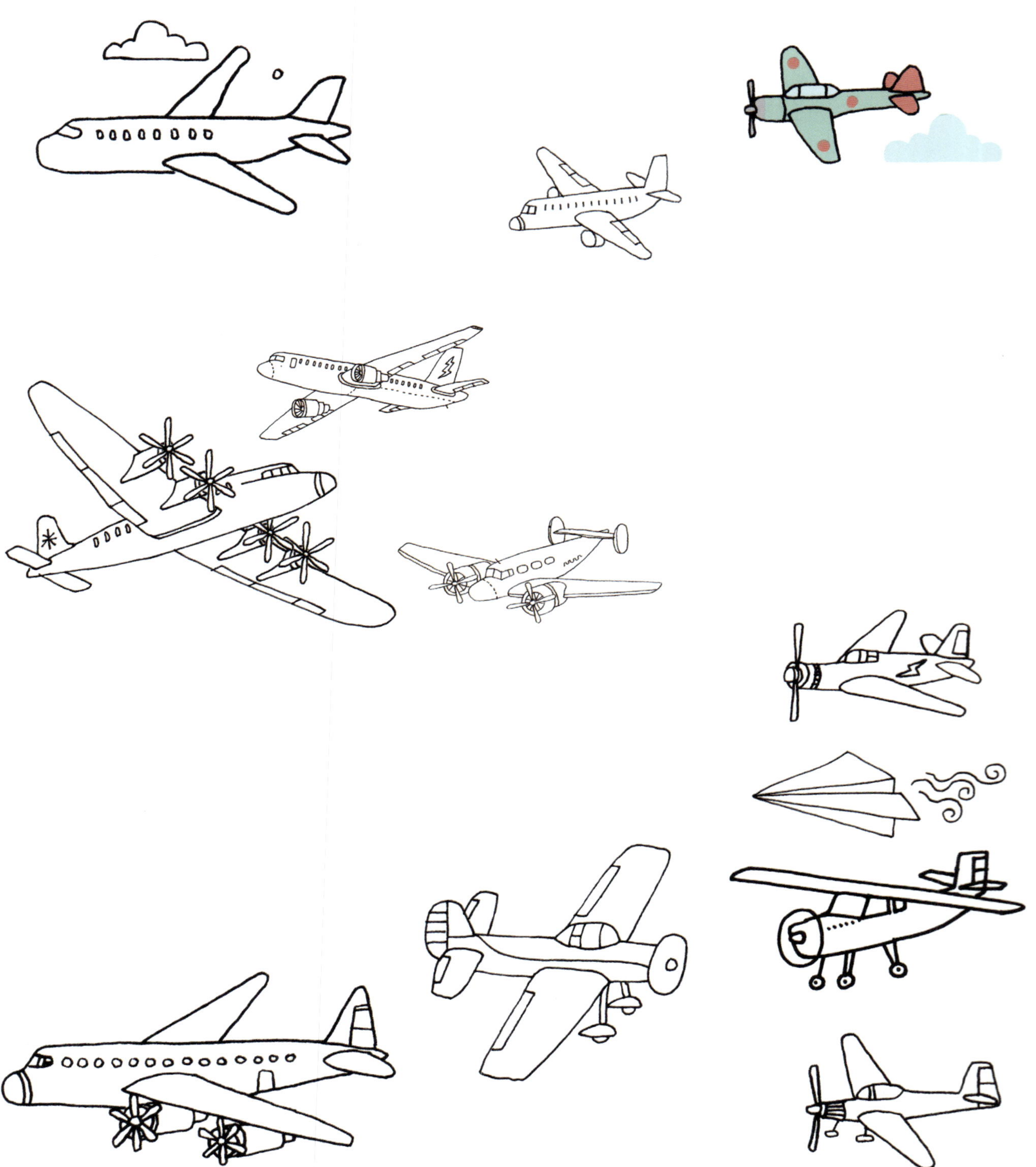

DRAW 20
jets and airplanes

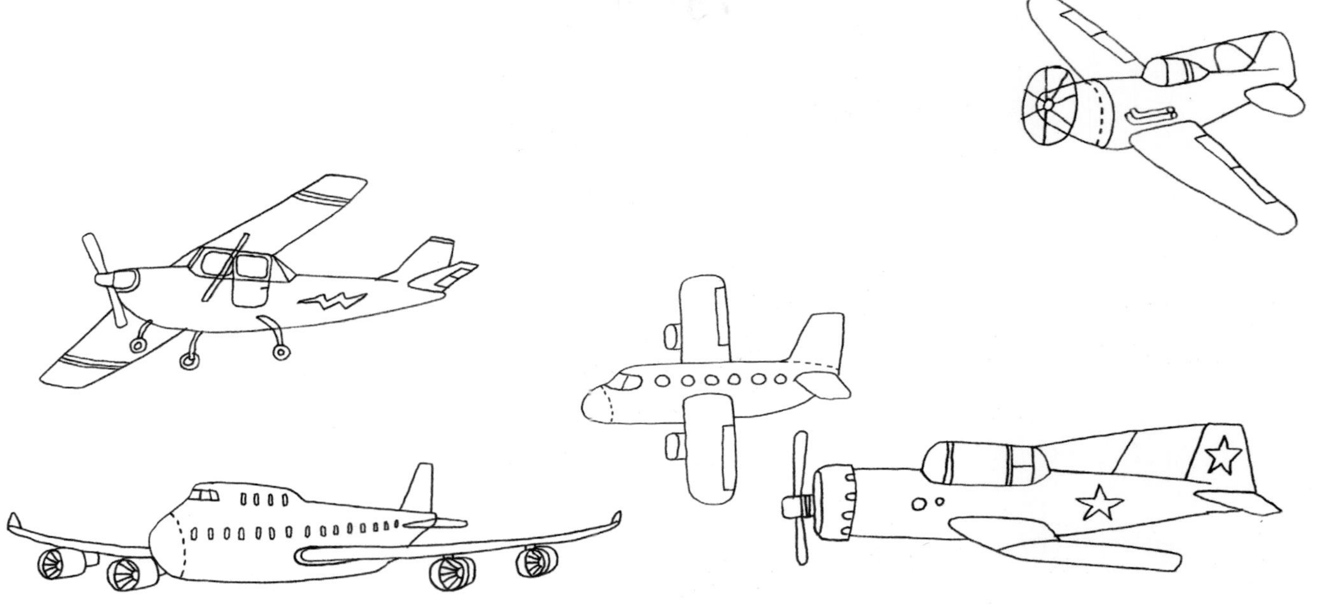

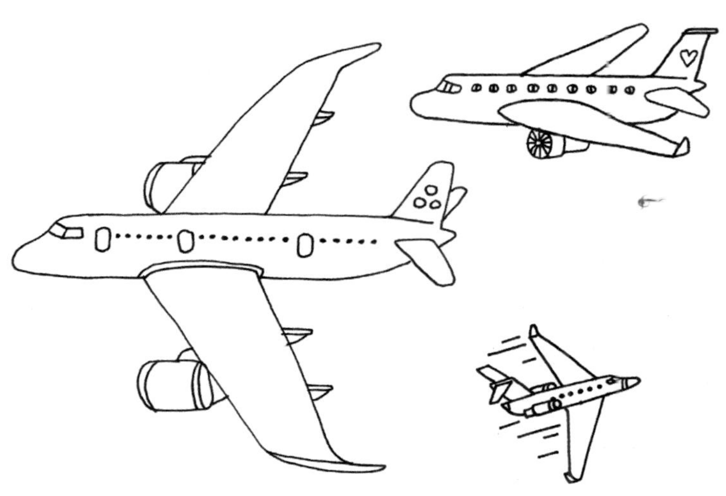

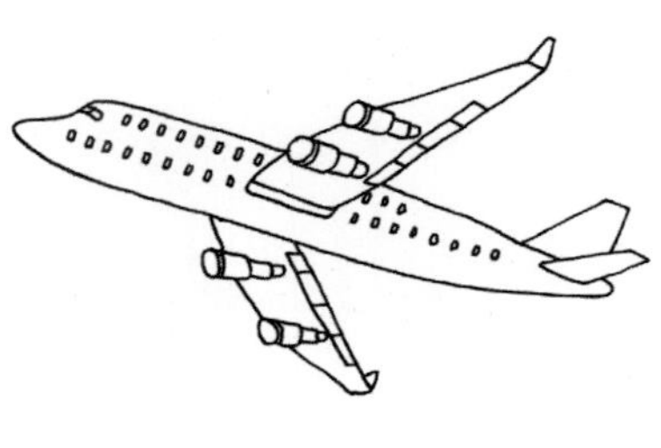

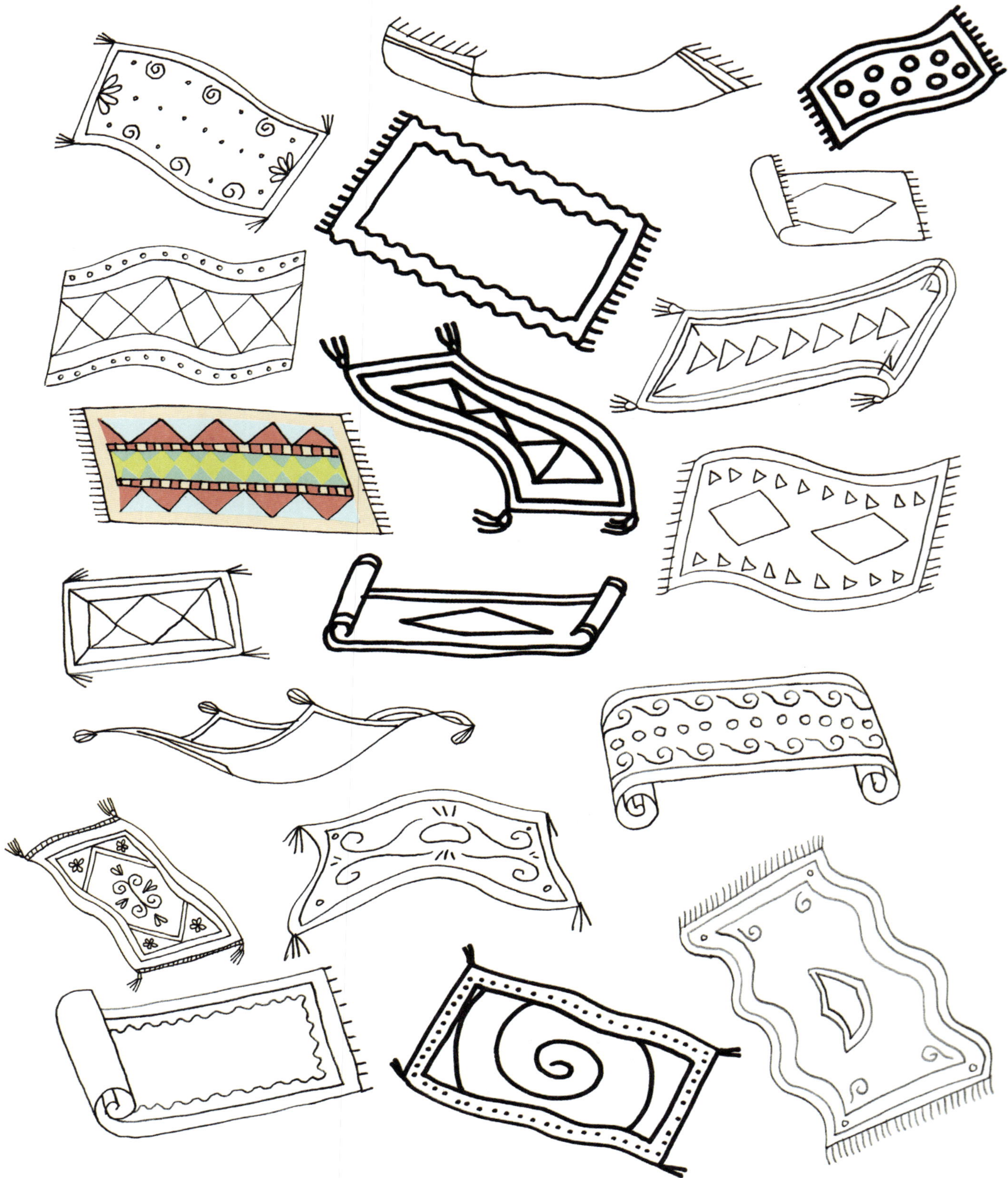

DRAW 20
MAGIC CARPETS

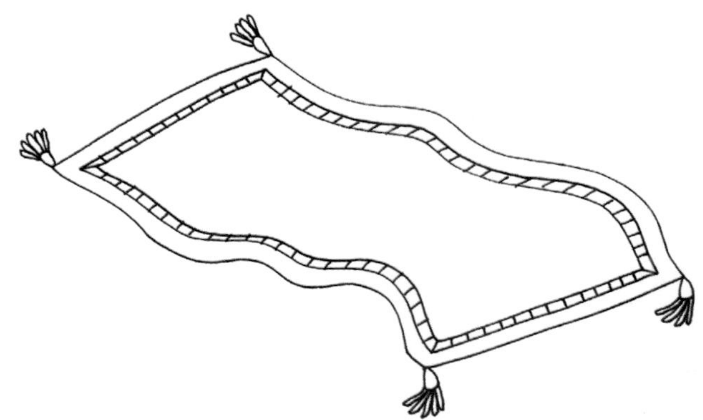

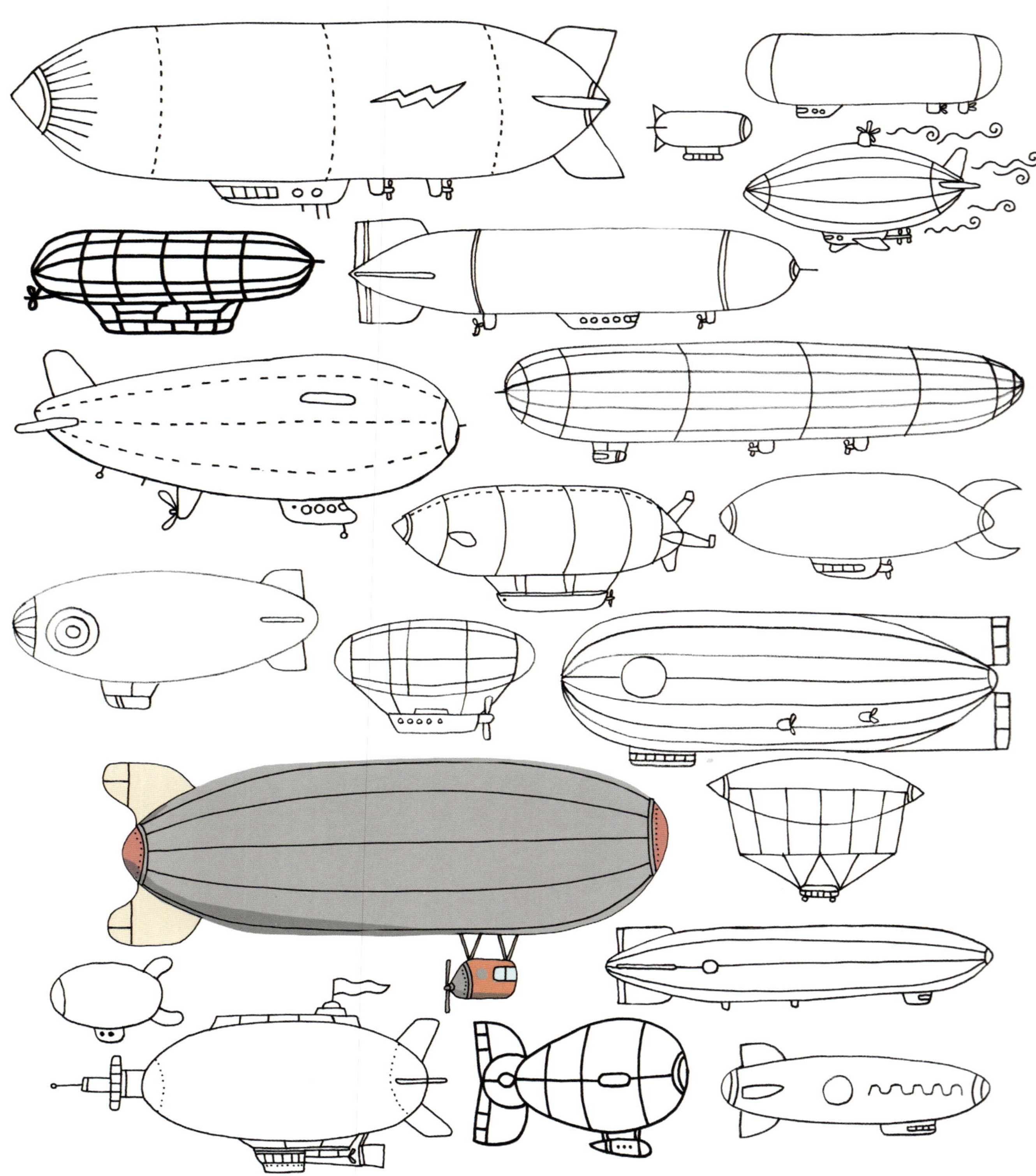

DRAW 20
Dirigibles

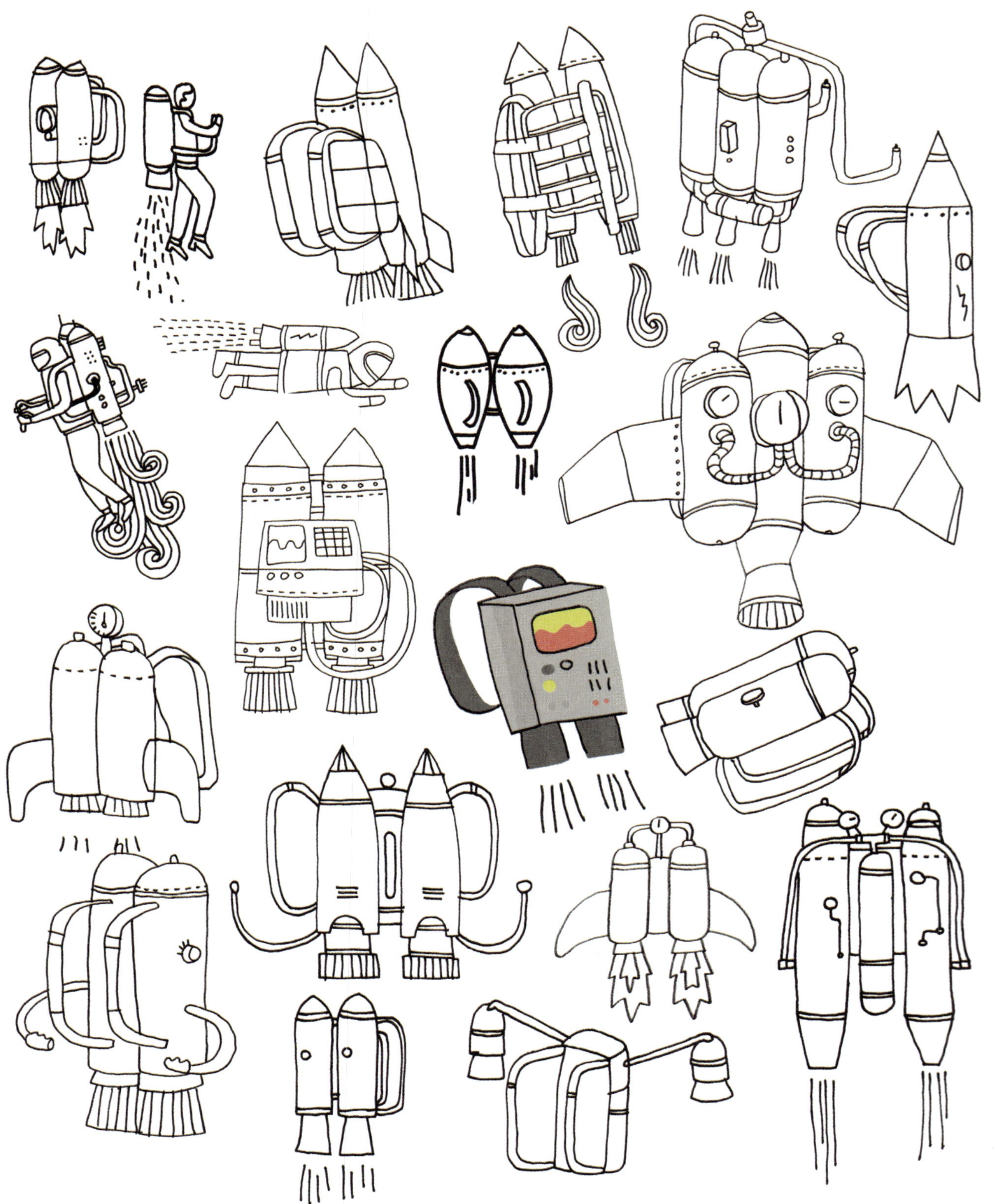

DRAW 20
Jet Packs

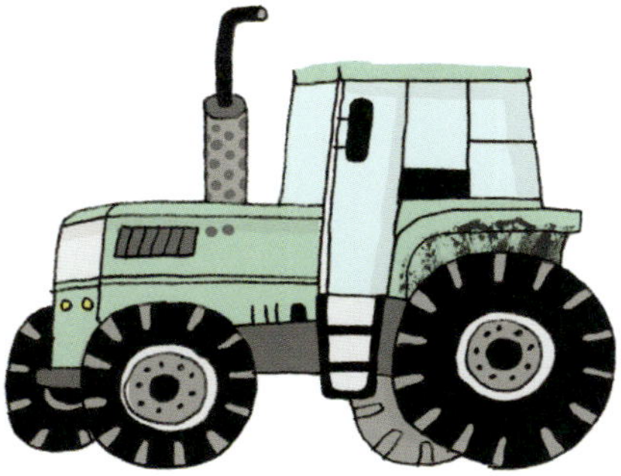

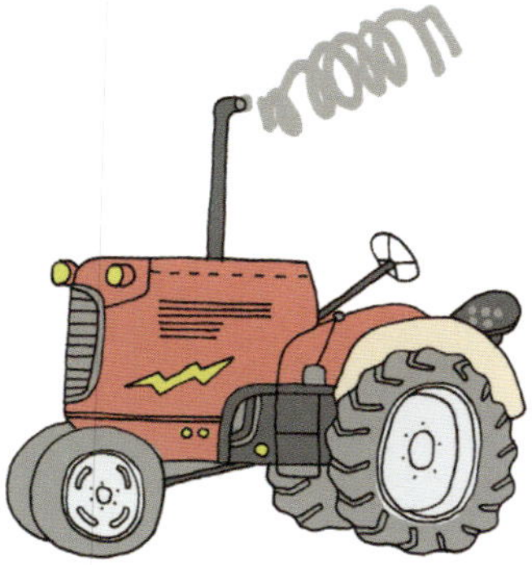

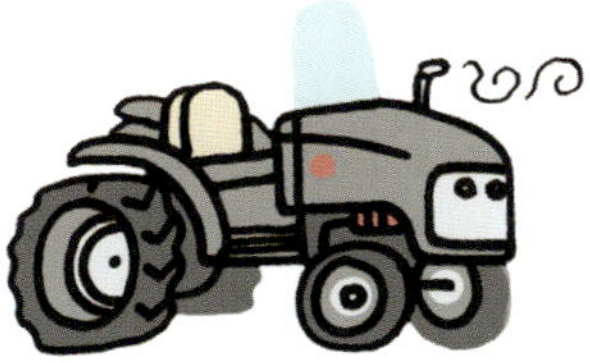

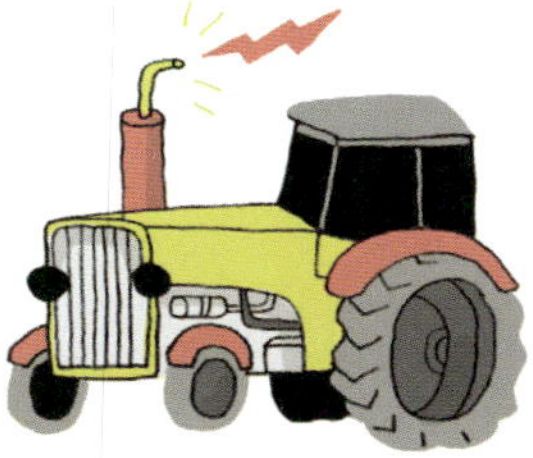

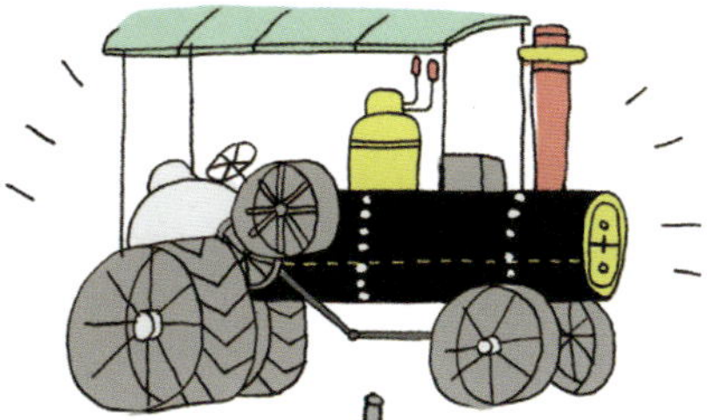

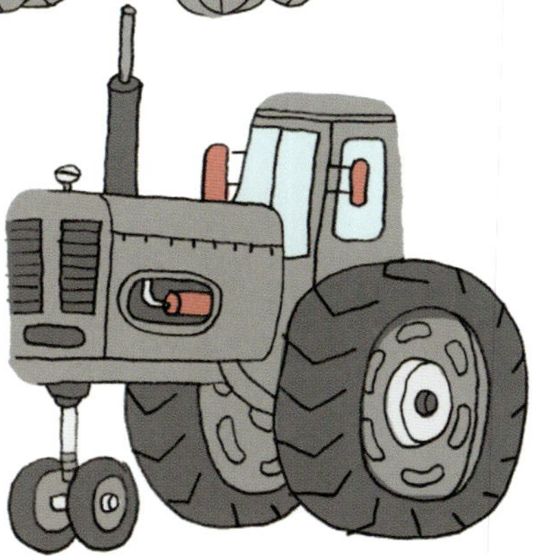

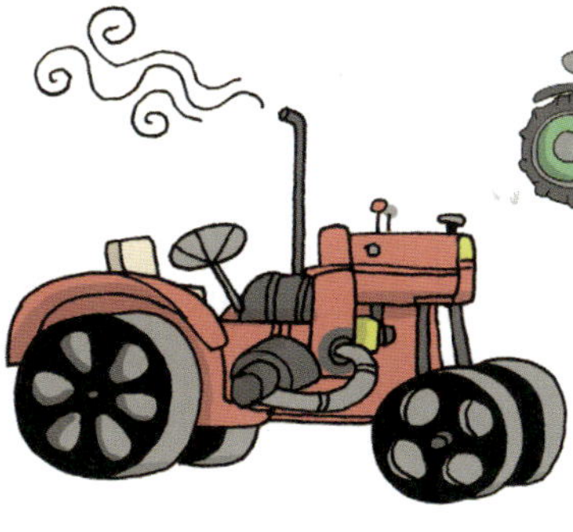

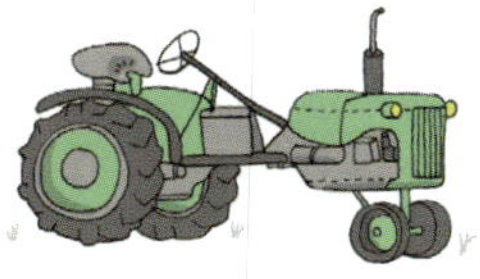

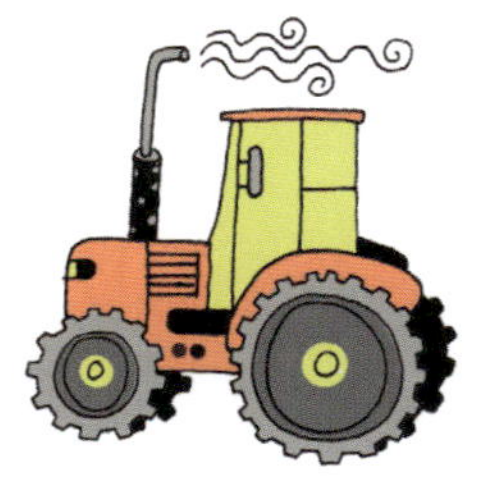
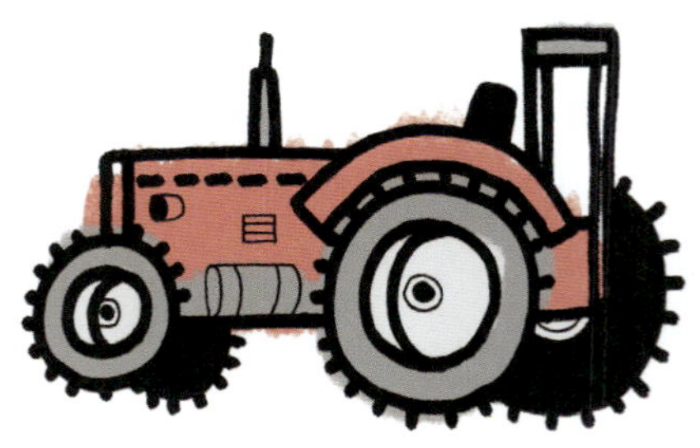
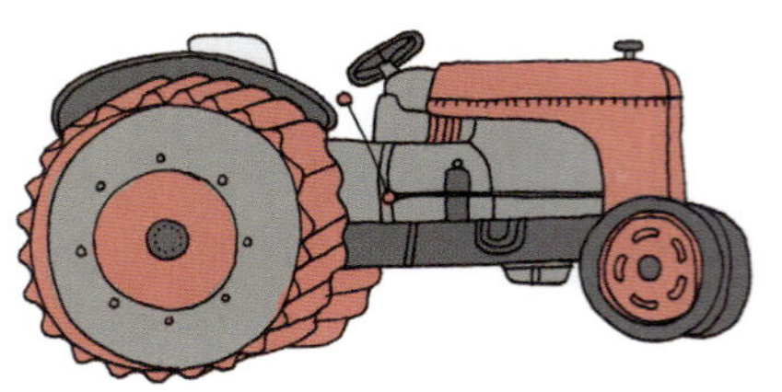
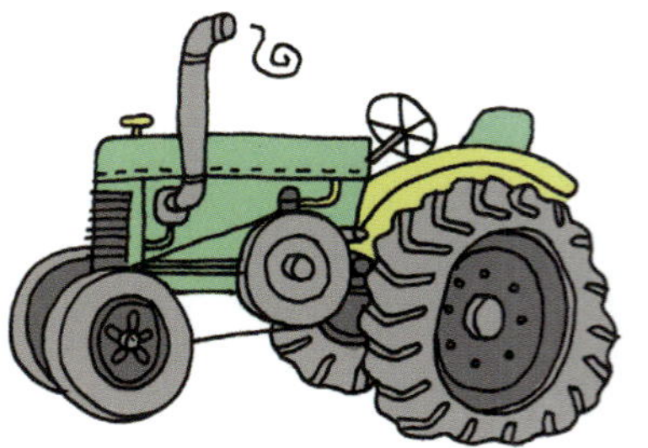

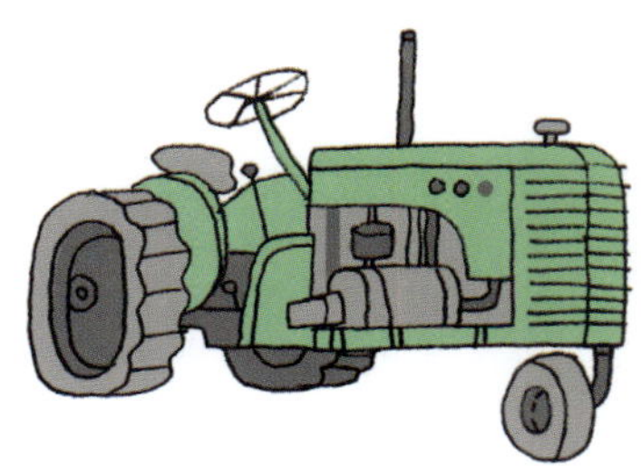

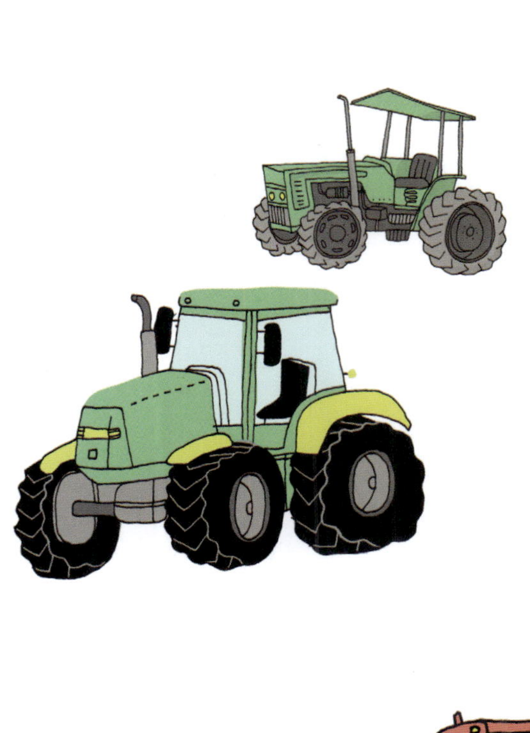

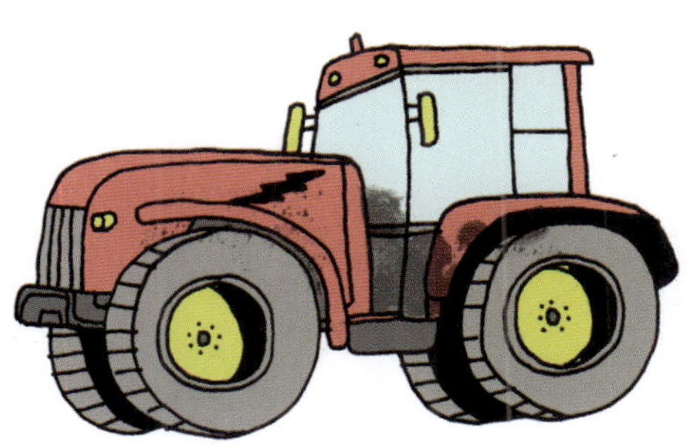

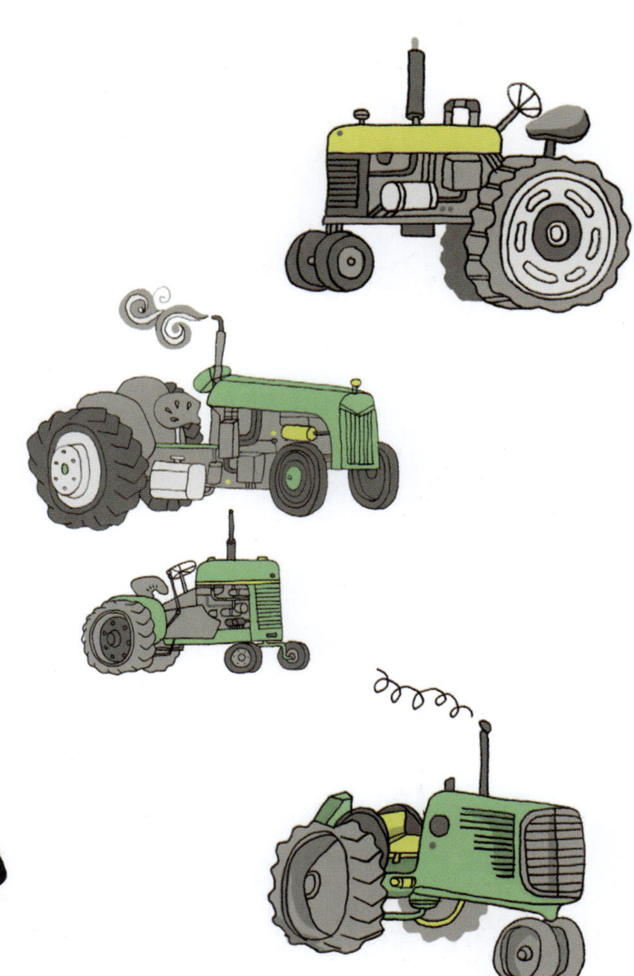

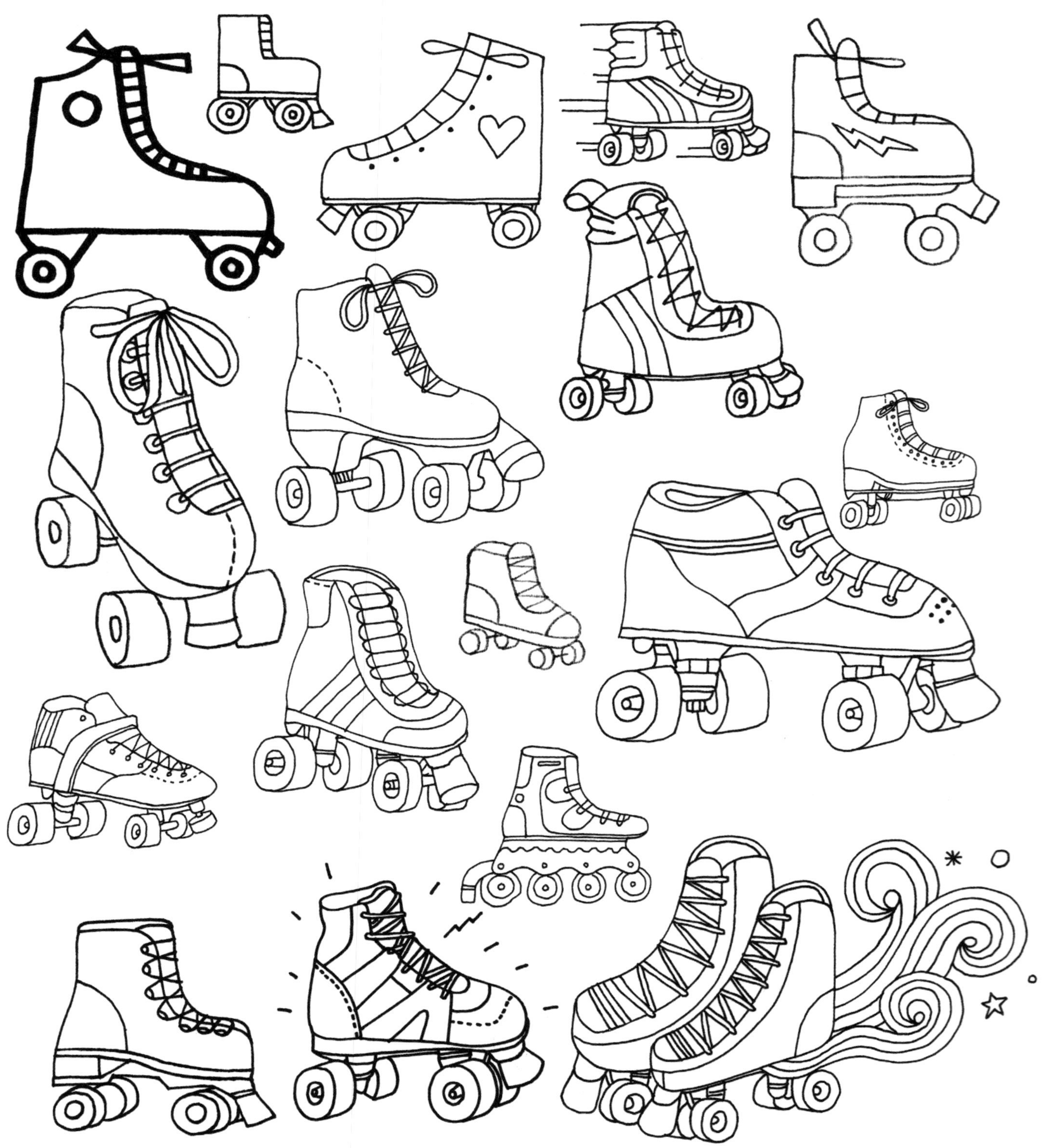

DRAW 20
ROLLER SKATES

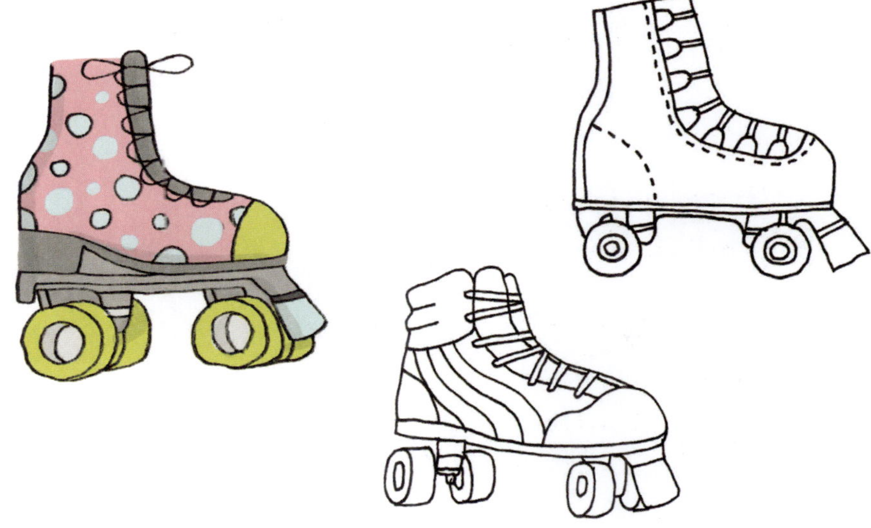

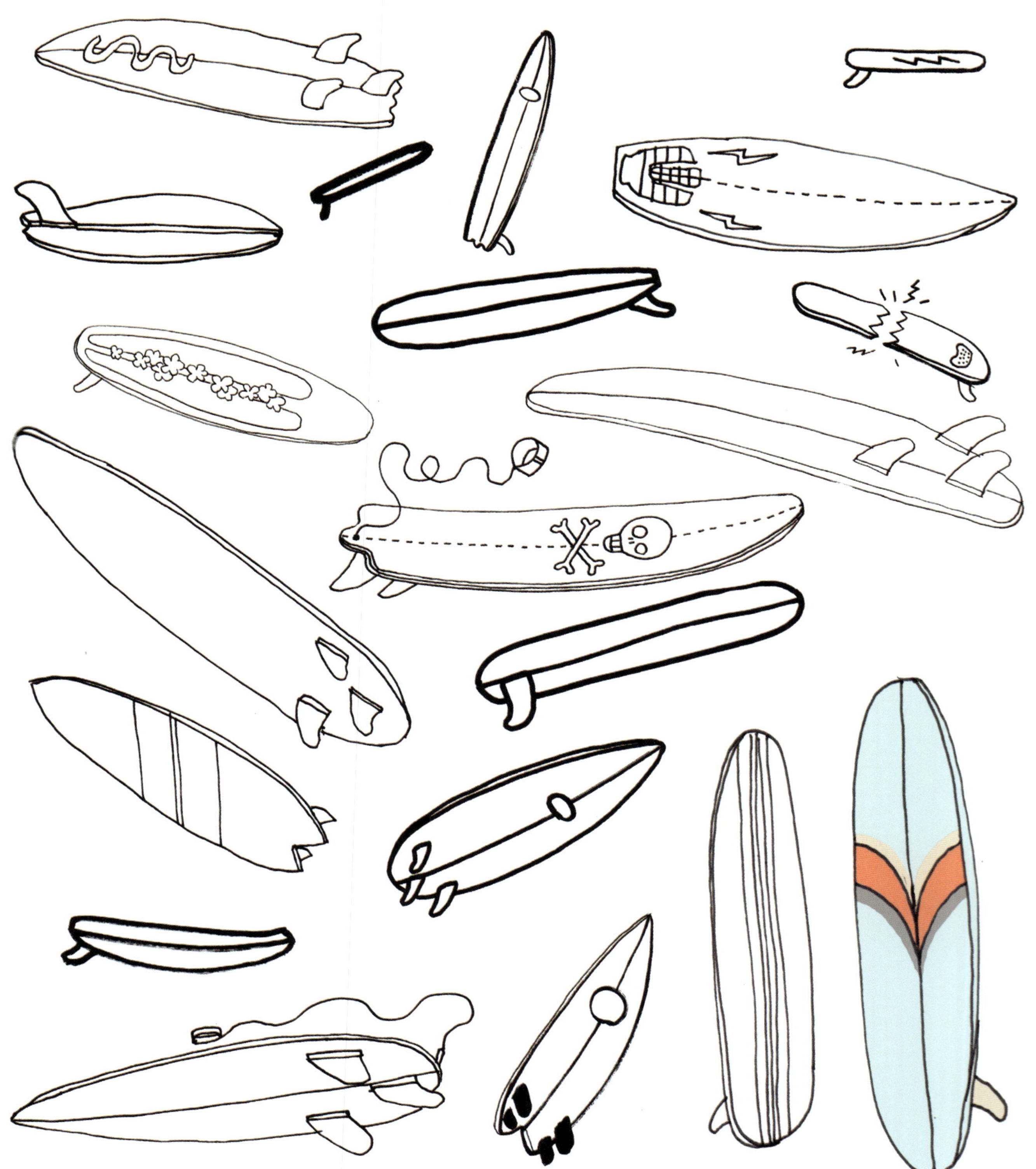

DRAW 20
Surfboards

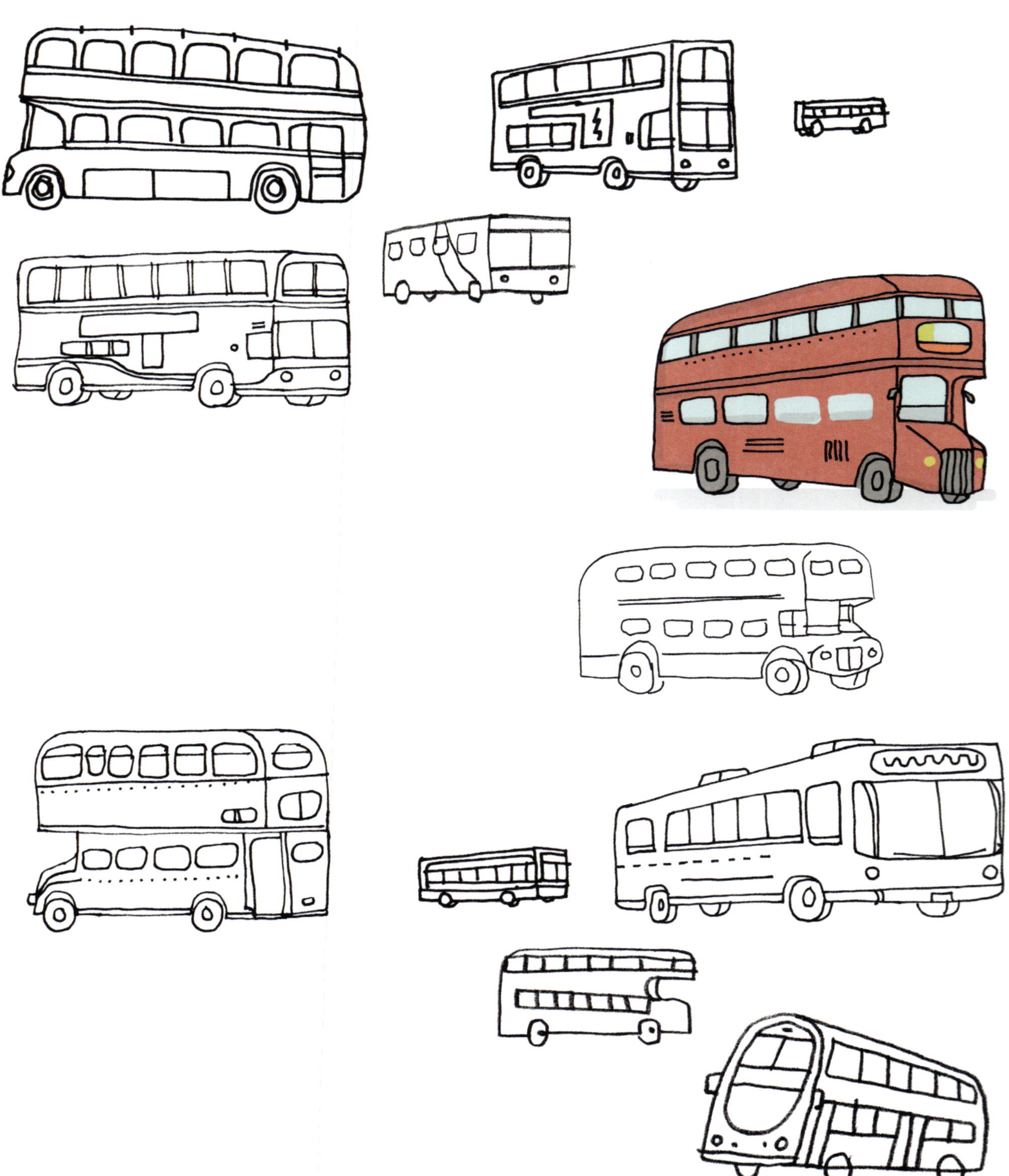

BUSES

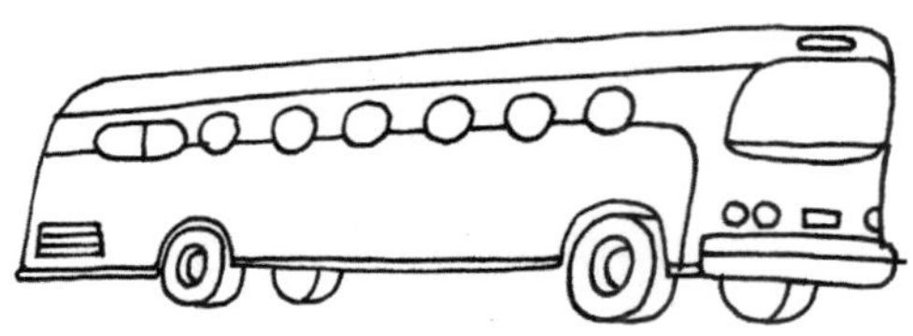

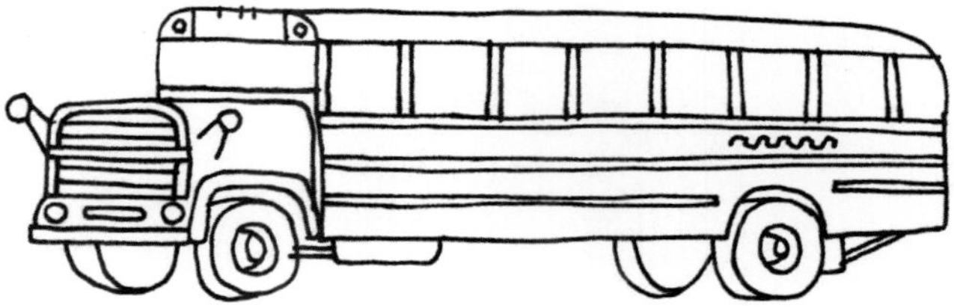

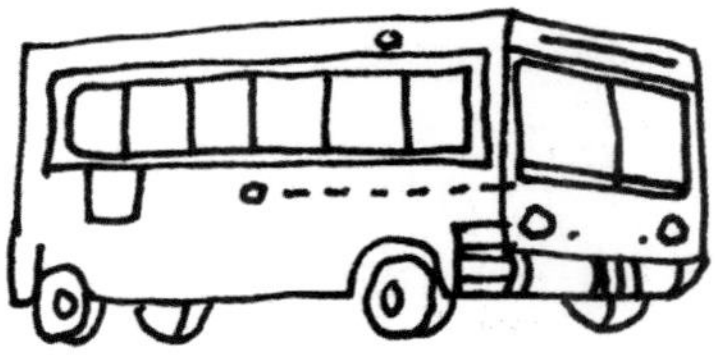

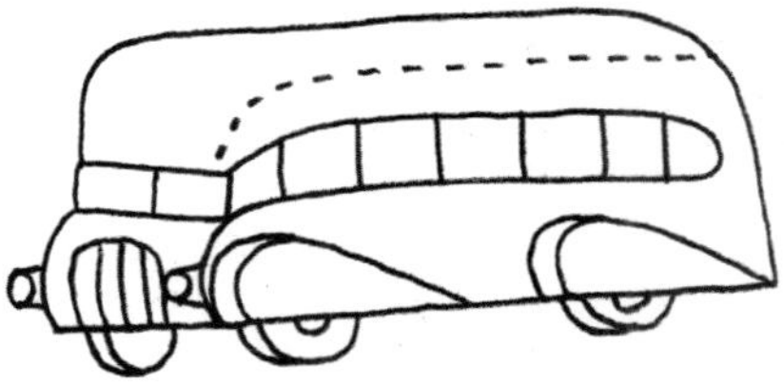

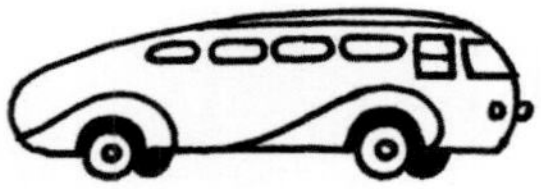

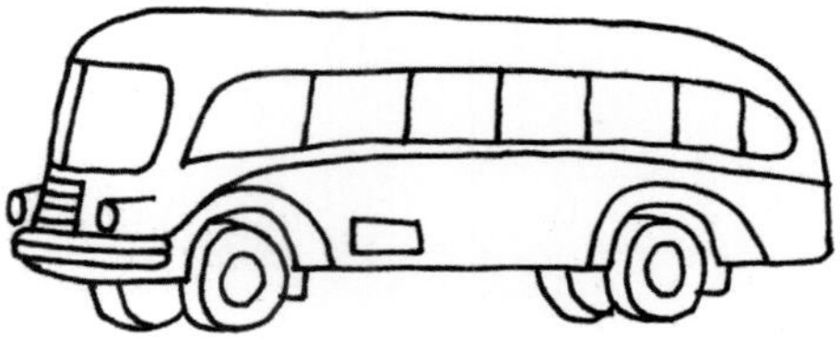

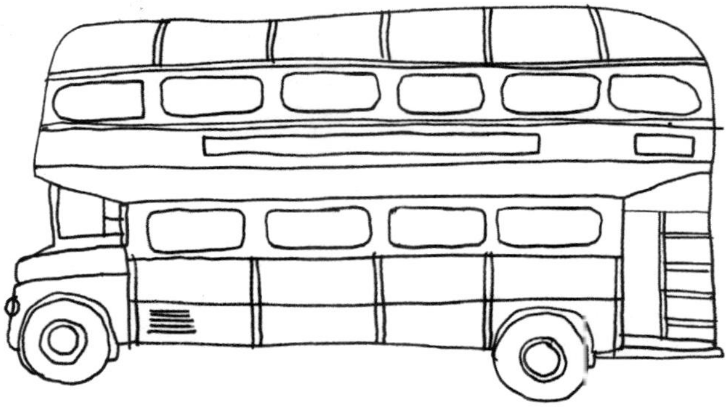

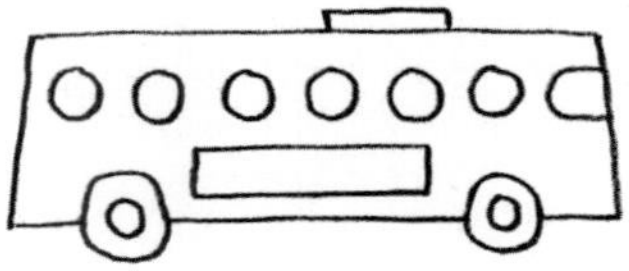

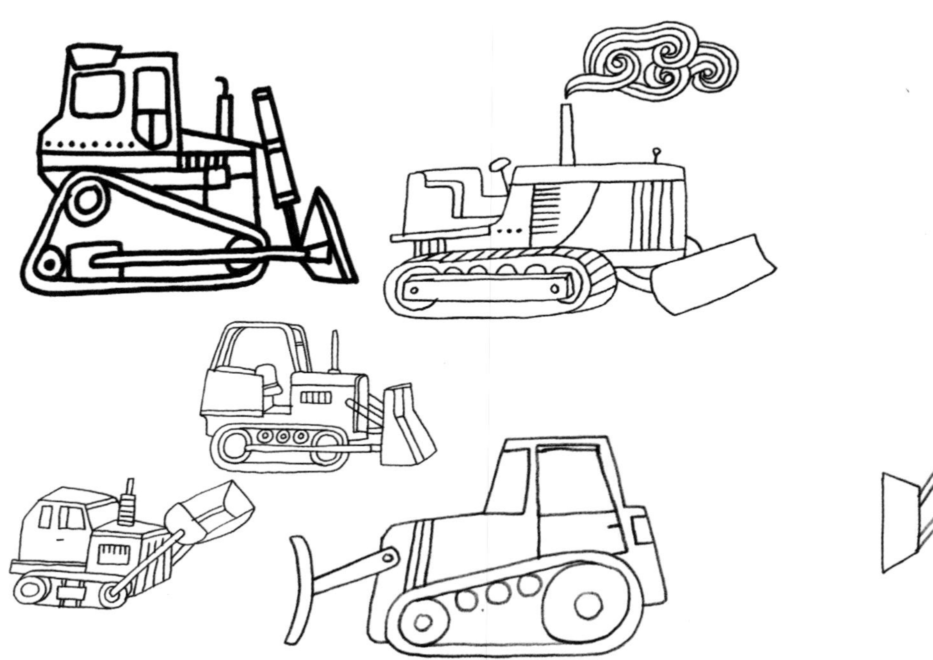

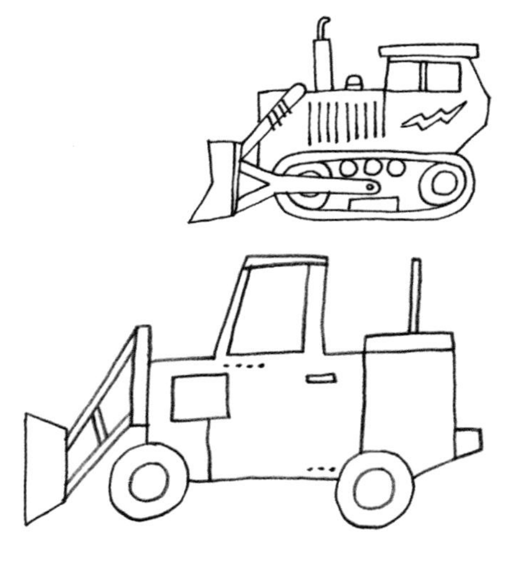

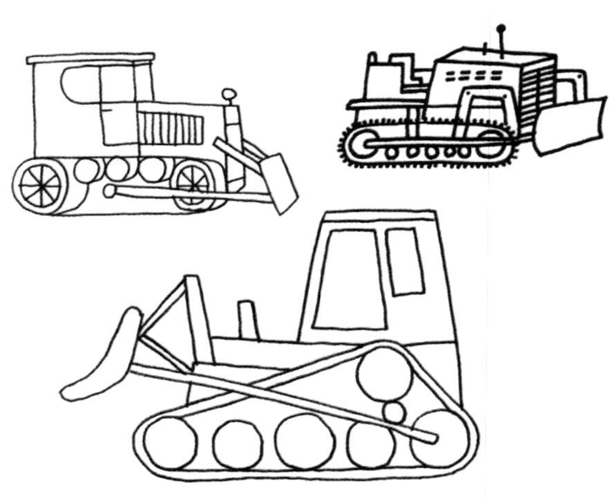

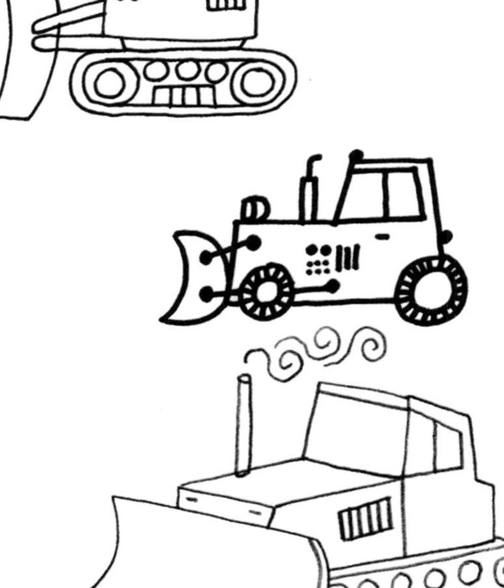

DRAW 20

bulldozers

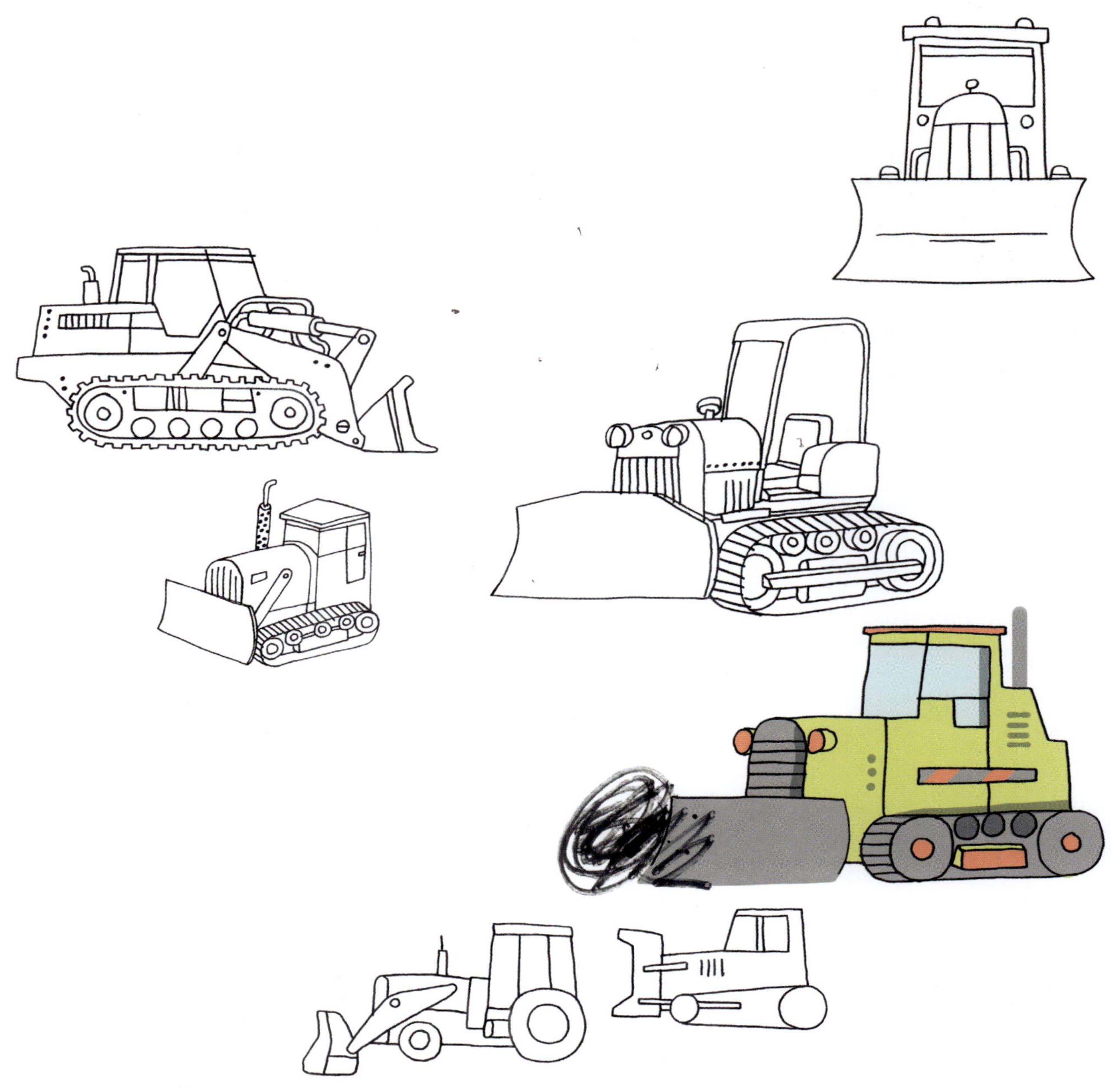

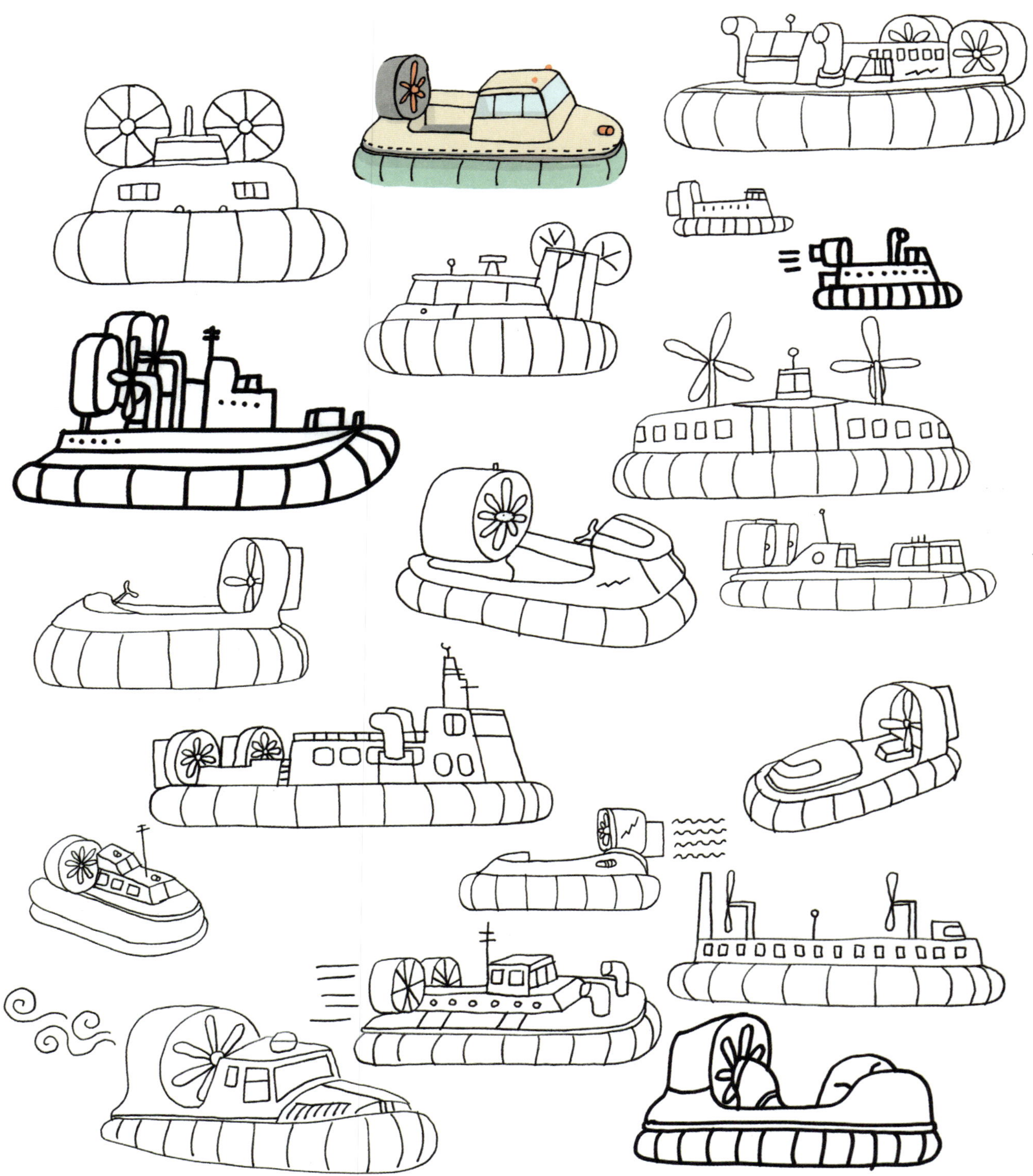

DRAW 20
Hovercraft

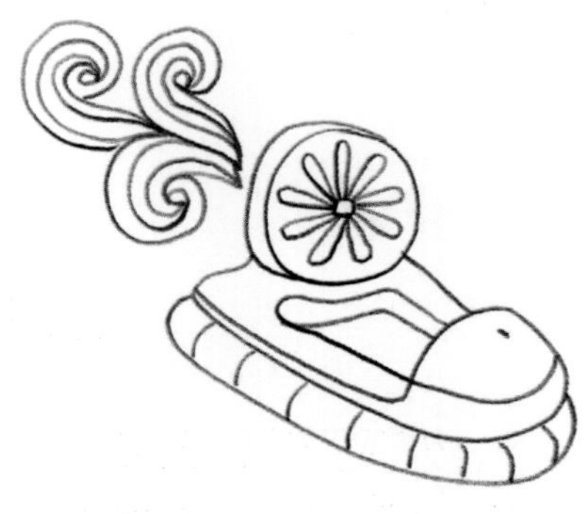

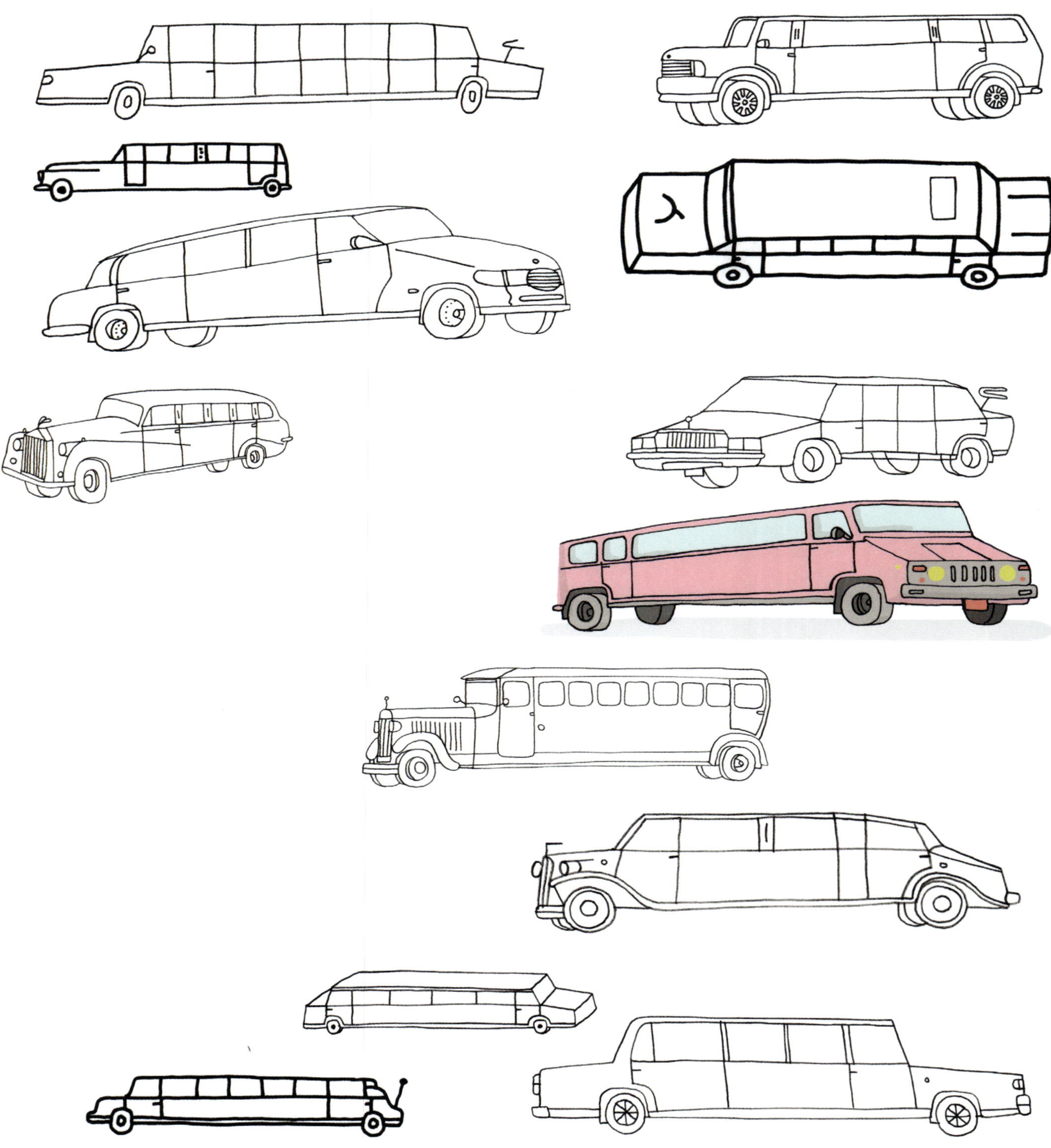

Limousines

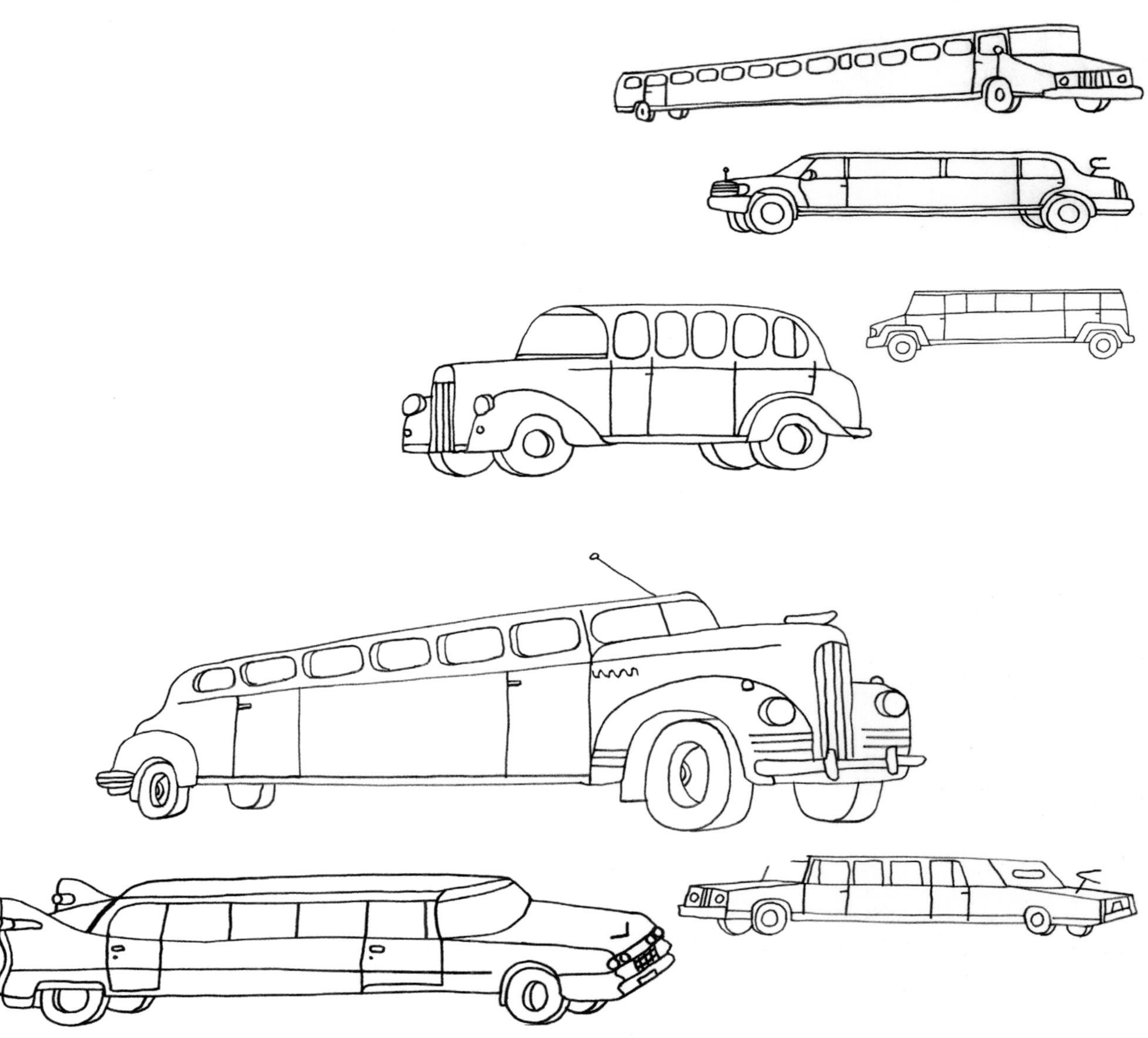

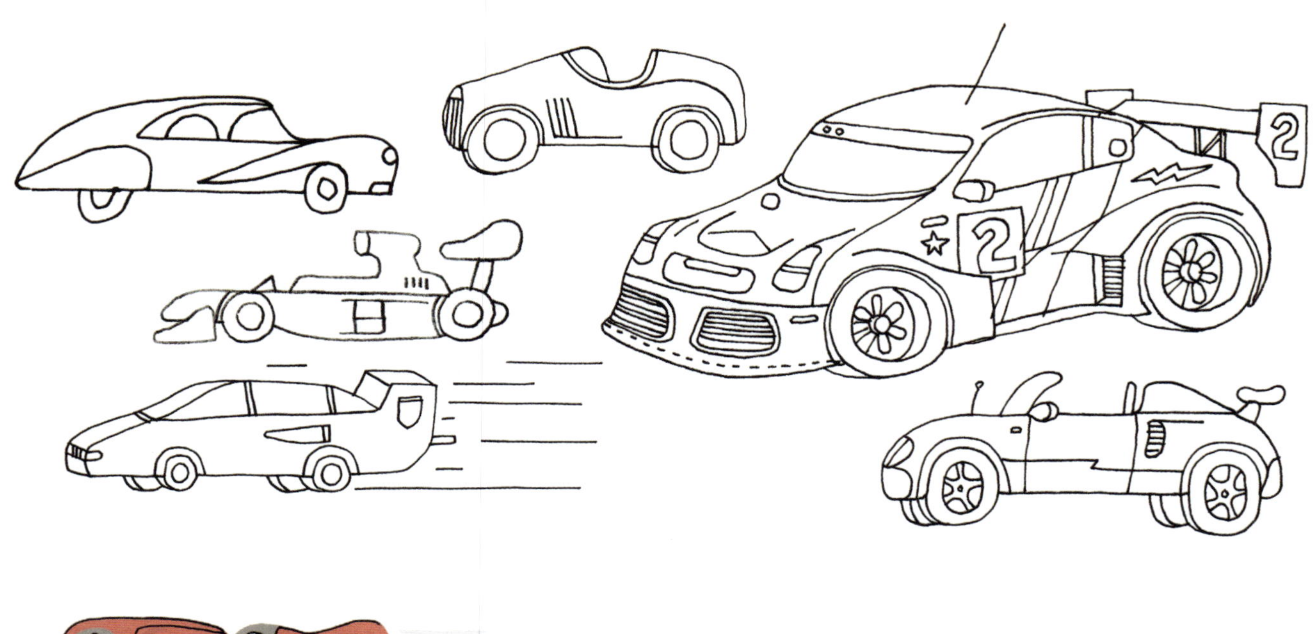

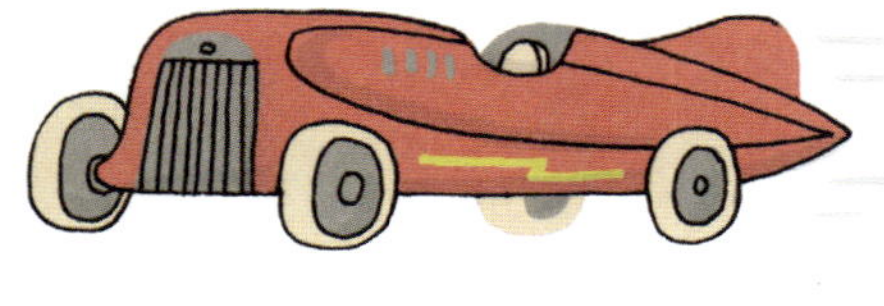

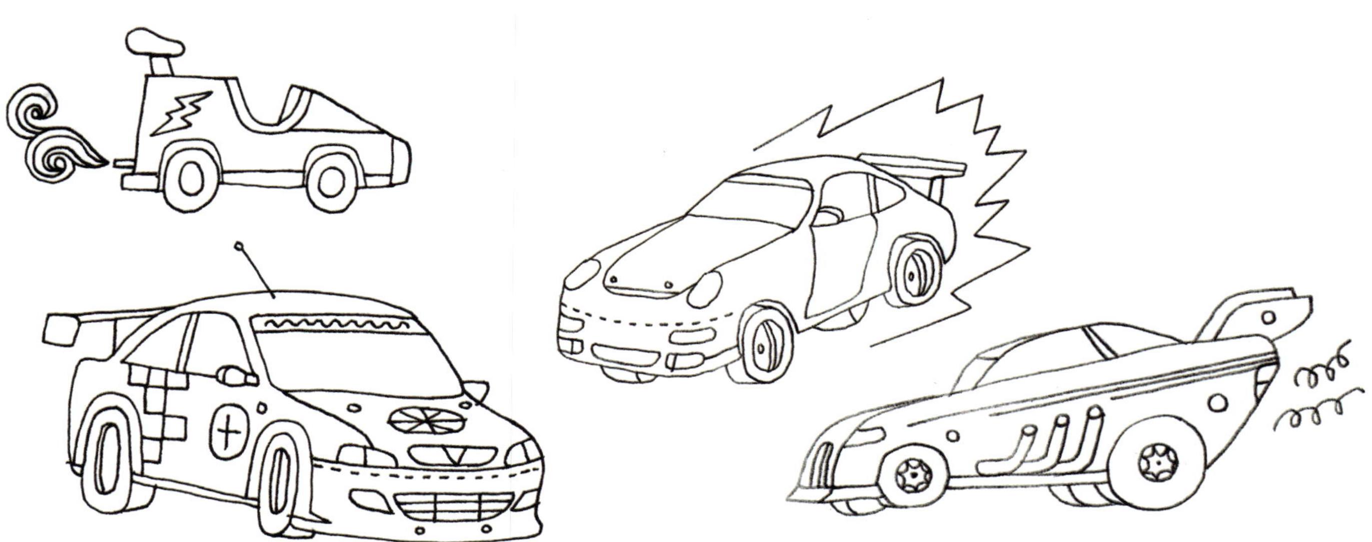

RACING CARS

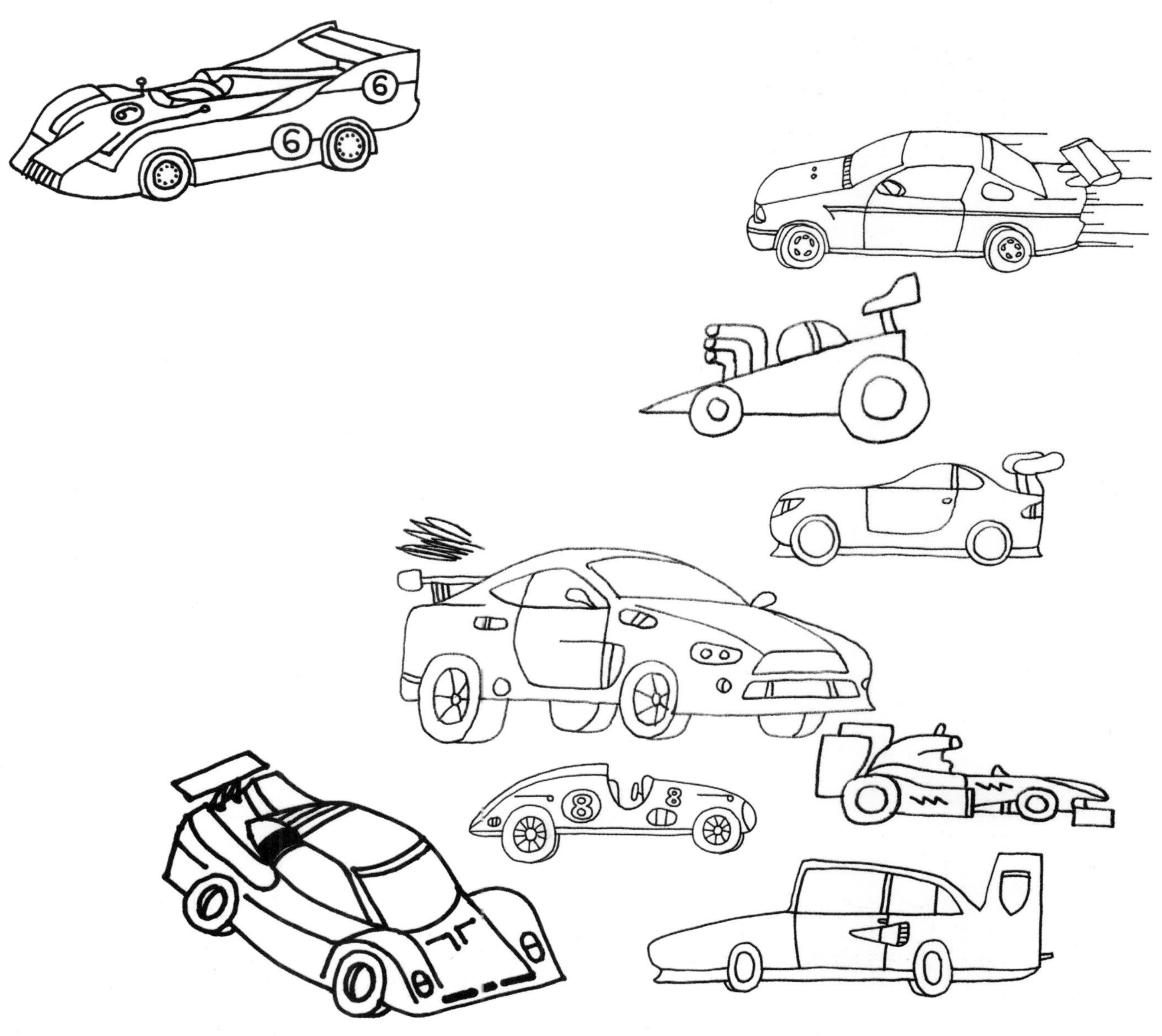

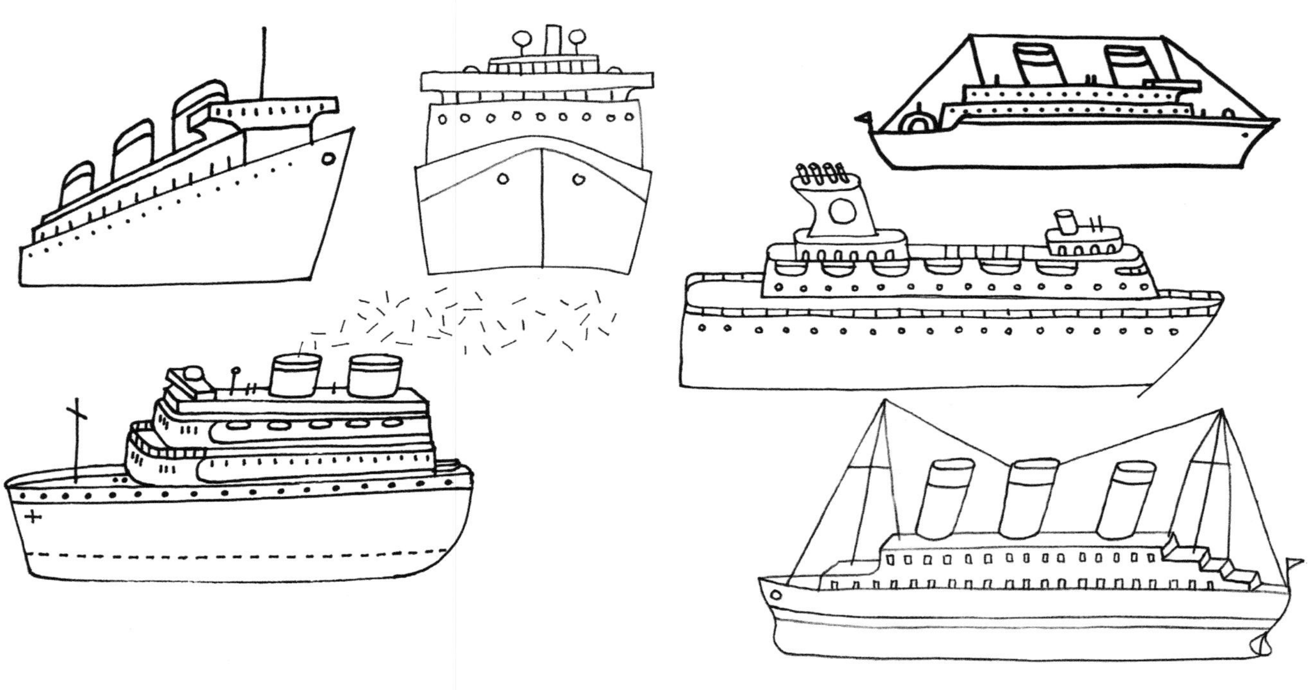

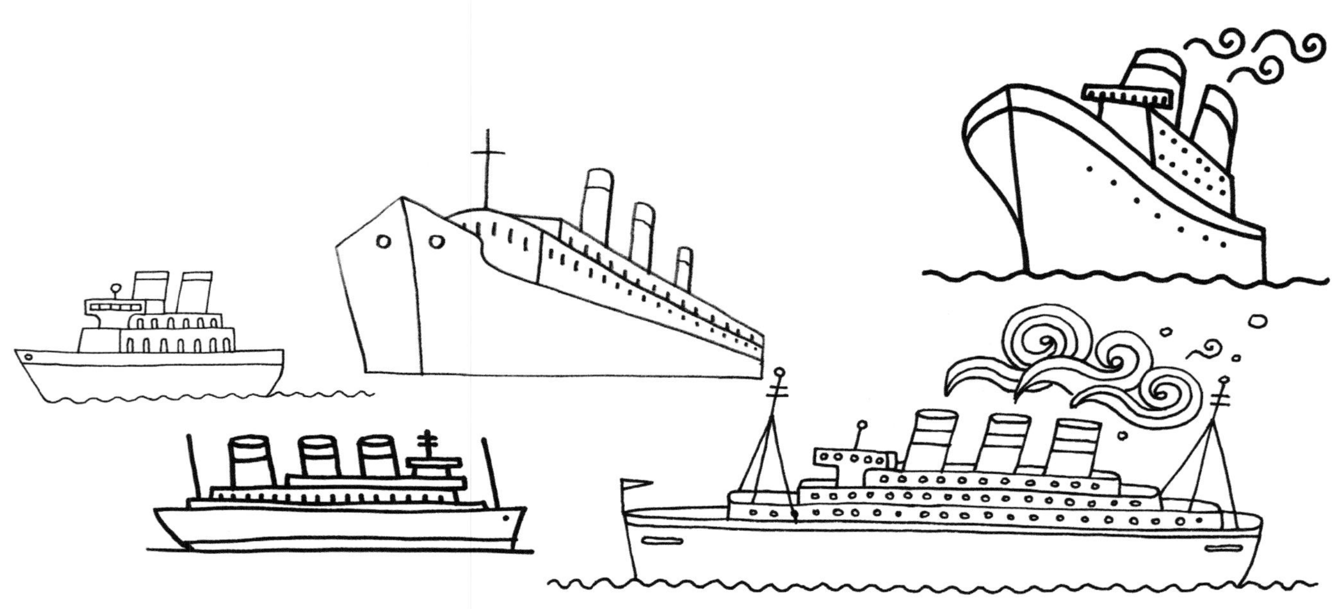

DRAW 20
OCEAN LINERS

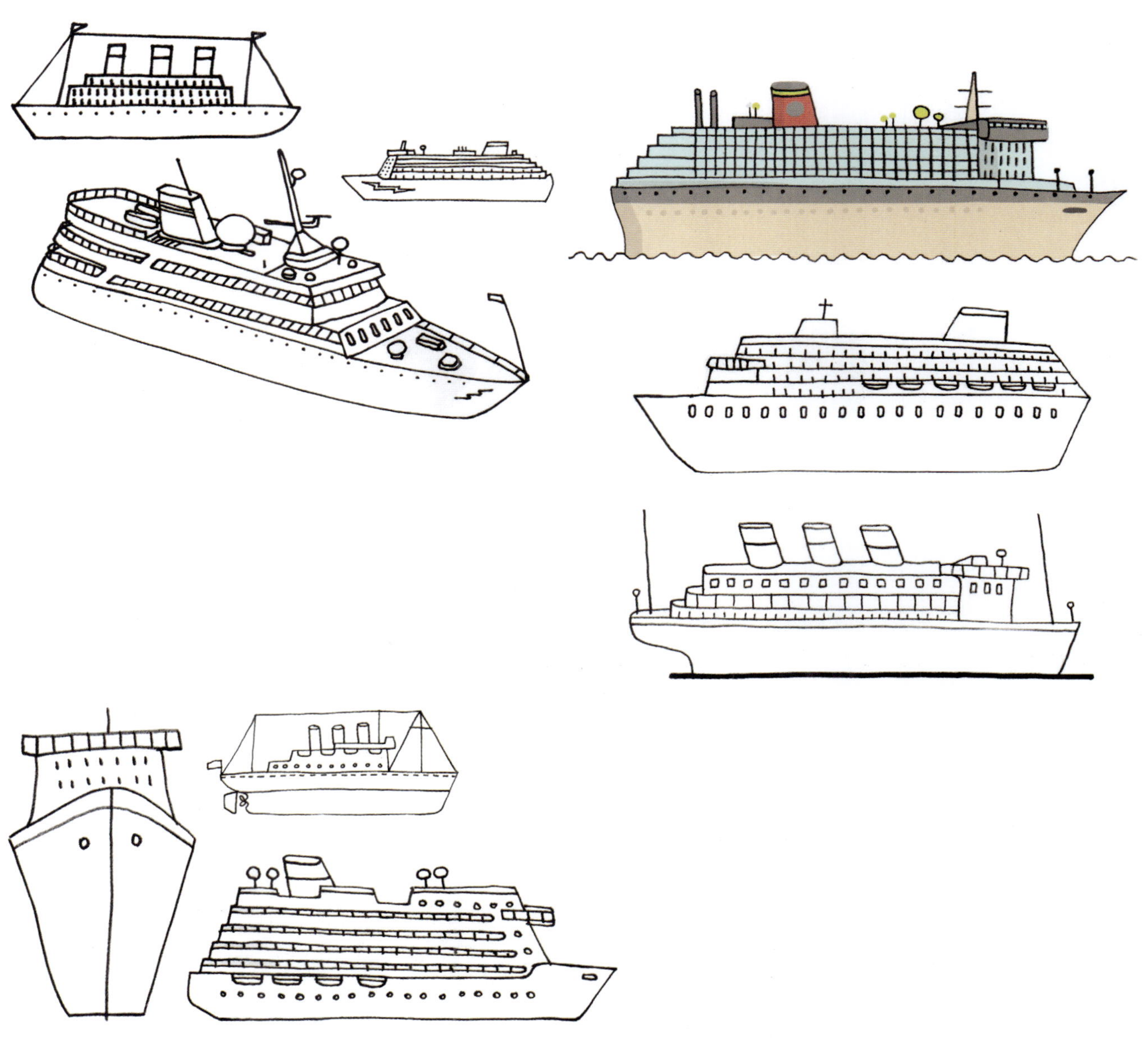

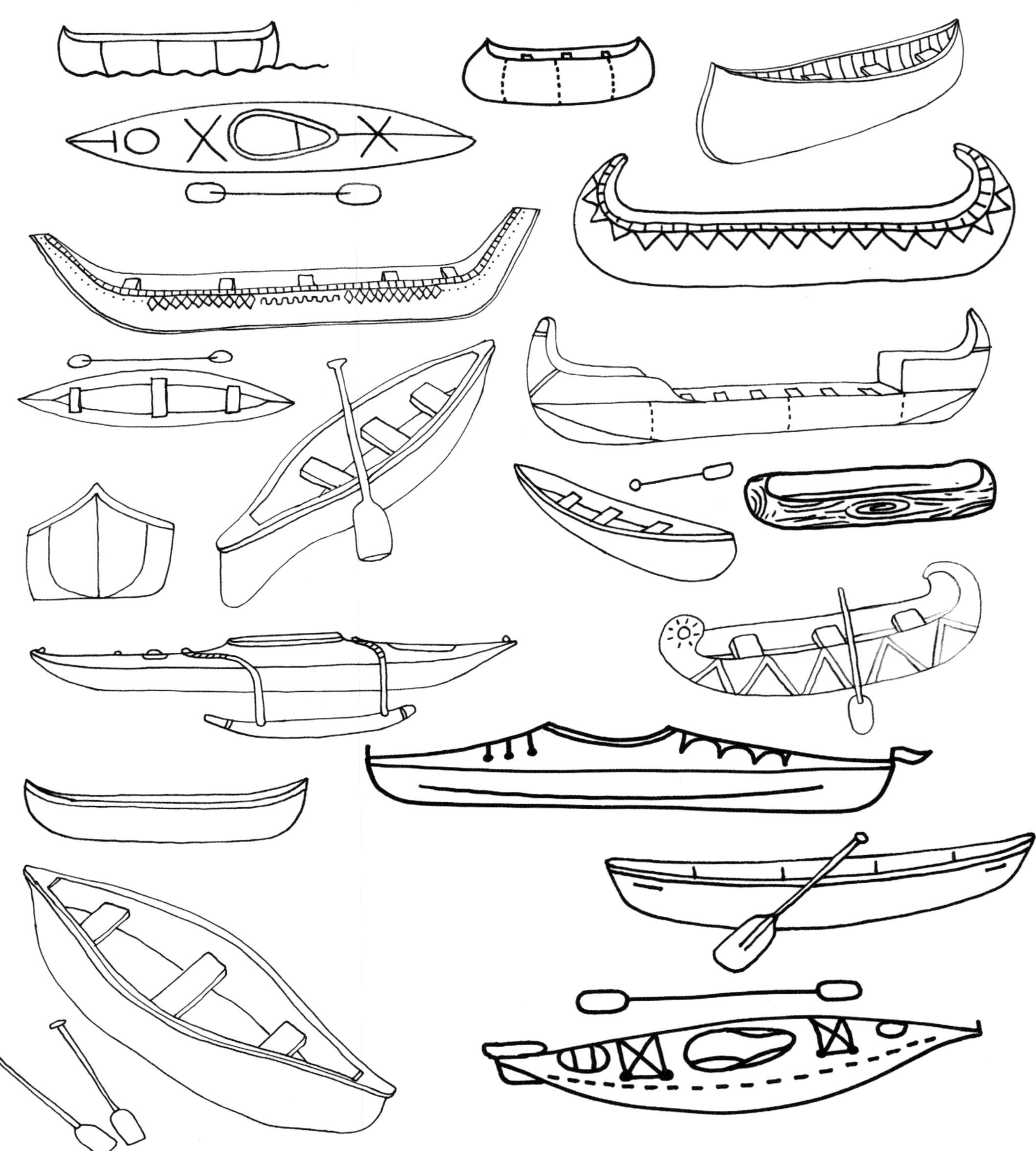

Canoes

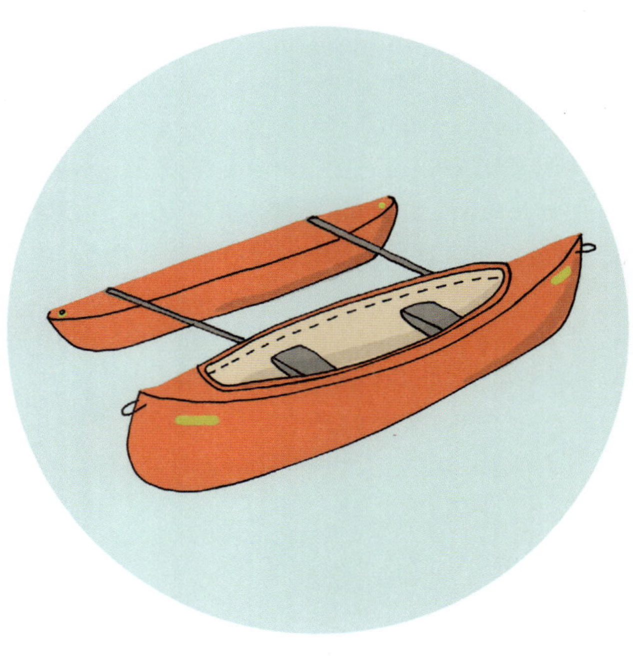

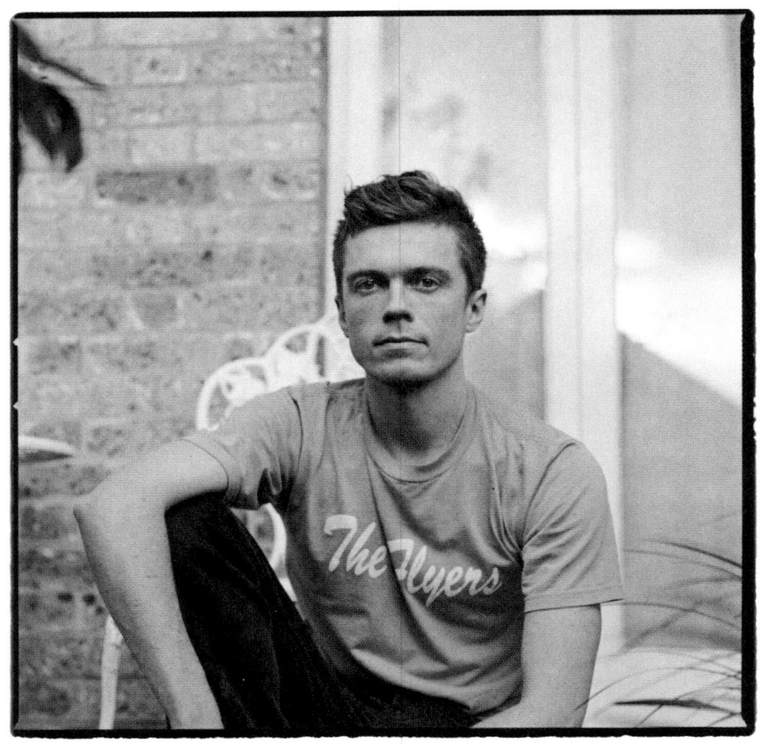

ABOUT THE ARTIST

James Gulliver Hancock is an international illustrator well known for his ambitious project, www.allthebuildingsinnewyork.com. Born in Sydney, Australia, James has lived all over the world, taking his whimsical perception to places such as Austria, Indonesia, the UK, France, and the USA. He studied visual communication in Sydney and is obsessed with drawing everything around him. *20 Ways to Draw a Bike* is a perfect fit for him as he feels everyone should draw the things around them to gain a fuller appreciation of the things they use every day. He lives between Sydney and Brooklyn and has a three-year-old son that is obsessed with anything with wheels—this one's for you, Quinn!

   You can see more of James's work at www.jamesgulliverhancock.com and www.allthebuildingsinnewyork.com.